ME→TO→WE

ME→TO→WE

The Shift Every Business Leader Must Make for Lasting Success

MICHAEL GUNTHER

PYP **Publish** Your Purpose

For permission requests, write to the publisher, addressed "Attention: Permissions Coordinator," at the address below.

Publish Your Purpose
141 Weston Street, #155
Hartford, CT, 06141

PYP **Publish** Your Purpose

The opinions expressed by the Author are not necessarily those held by Publish Your Purpose.

Ordering Information: Quantity sales and special discounts are available on quantity purchases by corporations, associations, and others. For details, contact the publisher at orders@publishyourpurposepress.com.

Edited by: Lori McFerran, Nancy Graham-Tillman
Cover design by: Nelly Murariu
Typeset by: Medlar Publishing Solutions Pvt Ltd., India

Printed in the United States of America.
ISBN: 978-1-955985-47-5 (hardcover)
ISBN: 978-1-955985-46-8 (paperback)
ISBN: 978-1-955985-45-1 (ebook)

Library of Congress Control Number: 2022902757

First edition, April 2022.

Publish Your Purpose is a hybrid publisher of non-fi c tion b ooks. Our authors are thought leaders, experts in their fi elds, and visionaries paving the way to social change—from food security to anti-racism. We give underrepresented voices power and a stage to share their stories, speak their truth, and impact their communities. Do you have a book idea you would like us to consider publishing? Please visit PublishYourPurpose. com for more information.

I dedicate this book to all the leaders and entrepreneurs whose persistence drives them to become exceptional guides for their teams, clients, and communities. I'm grateful to the thousands of inspiring leaders and clients who allowed me to be part of their leadership journey.

CONTENTS

CONCLUSION
THE ROAD AHEAD 255

CHAPTER 1

TRIPPED UP

If you're an entrepreneur or business leader, you've been there. Probably more than once. I'm guessing you've experienced a disastrous, soul-crushing, "chuck-it-all" moment—like my Christmas Eve in 2012.

The day started out fine. For the first time in years, I'd finished my holiday shopping early. My husband, Steve, had just placed a prime rib in the oven. I uncorked a favorite pinot noir from a nearby Paso Robles winery. We planned to spend the afternoon relaxing at the house with his mother. That's when I received an urgent phone call from my landlord.

Our office building had been tented for termite remediation despite a series of storms that soaked the area. Instead of removing the tents, the termite company allowed four feet of water to accumulate on the flat roof, creating a giant kiddie pool. Doubling down on dumb, they then cut holes in the tent rather than pump the water off the roof.

The water raced to find the nearest escape routes—the air vents, which emptied right into my company's headquarters. This included Steve's real estate office too, as we shared space.

"Don't let them move anything," I said to my landlord, worrying the termite company would do even more damage. "We'll be there in 10 minutes." Steve turned off the oven and told his mom we'd eat a bit later.

When I opened the office door, I knew most of the contents inside were beyond rescue, including soaked computers and drenched hard files. The sheetrock walls looked like giant sponges with Rorschach test water stains. Despite my plea to the contrary, the workers had stacked equipment on desks, ripped up the carpet, and pulled wires from the wall. A decade's worth of work had been washed away.

The stench of mold and mildew had already begun to take over. *Good luck getting anyone to come help with computer backup until after the holidays*, I told myself. Steve's office shared the same soggy state. *Where is anyone going to work? This isn't an office; it's a hurricane zone.*

I implored the workers not to move anything else. I wanted the insurance company to see the disaster as-is, praying the termite company's policy covered indoor floods. *How long until I can get a settlement? A month? A year? Ever?*

Driving home I felt an intense and rapidly changing spin cycle of emotions. I lashed out at the termite company. *Who allows water to drain through air vents?!* I kicked myself, knowing I should've backed up my computers recently and stored the data elsewhere, and I panicked about client materials and our accounting files. I felt overwhelmed and demoralized about the months of catch-up work ahead and wanted to crawl into a warm bed and make it all go away.

Then I had a new thought: Maybe the flooding was a sign to shutter my business. For good. You see, the water wasn't the most frustrating part of the year. Far from it.

My company, Collaboration LLC, a business consulting firm headquartered on the Central Coast of California, had experienced some initial success but had stagnated of late. We had been in business for 10 years, but I felt like I was still running a startup.

As CEO, I knew the onus rested on me, and I felt like I was making the same rookie mistakes over and over. I struggled to articulate a clear vision for our firm of 13 employees. Shoot, I couldn't even outline a clear vision in my head. I "chased sexy," veering from opportunity to opportunity rather than focusing on what we did best and sticking to that. I thought I was a decent communicator, but a series of lost clients, employees, and business partners started to convince me otherwise.

I felt isolated and lonely. I bit my lip whenever outsiders praised the firm as an exemplary success. *If they only knew.* I desperately wanted to ask for guidance but didn't have any business colleagues in whom I could confide. Business consulting firms that offer help can't ever ask for it!

A decade into my business and I was still receiving the lowest pay of all the staff, working the longest hours (Weekends? What's a weekend?) and setting new records for stress creation and anxiety consumption. *You're a fraud*, I told myself. *If people knew how you ran your own business, they'd never hire you.* I wanted to quit right there. I wanted to give notice...to myself.

Instead, with my shoes and pants still soaked from the flooding, I had another, slightly less drastic idea—flee the country.

Steve and I had been fantasizing about taking a two-week trip to Europe in the spring. I wanted to go right then! For as long as possible. Bank accounts be damned! As Steve attempted to rescue the prime rib and the rest of our dinner, I rambled on about Mediterranean beaches and three-hour lunches.

Maybe it was the wine or the allure of no alarm clocks. It definitely wasn't the overcooked prime rib. But by the end of the evening, Steve and I hatched a crazy idea to expand our two-week vacation we had planned for September of the coming year into an eight-week sabbatical. We'd cash out every frequent flier mile and max out the credit cards. At that moment, I didn't care about our finances (or lack thereof). I needed out. I didn't even care about the fate of my business. *If it fails while I'm gone, it fails. I'll find another career. I hope.*

As the sabbatical approached, I didn't spend a lot of time training my staff to take over during my absence or give them instructions on how to carry out my responsibilities. If they couldn't handle it, c'est la vie. I was spent and beyond my breaking point. I knew I couldn't continue. Half of my brain wanted the operation to fail in my absence. Anything is better than the status quo.

My troubles continued to pile up. The insurance money remained elusive, and several clients decided to stop paying their bills. I worried about having enough money to pay for meals in Europe. Thank God we booked flights and hotels with travel points.

On the way to the airport, I thought about my mother, who had passed away a year prior. She would've celebrated the trip. To her final day, she remained a huge fan of travel, of adventure, of embracing the big ol' world of opportunity around us. With 17 kids (yes, 17!), she learned to stop trying to plan every inch of life and instead enjoy it. She fed her mind, body, and soul with good books, exotic foods, and long hugs. When I wavered about the trip, I thought about her and continued forward.

I looked over at Steve, my partner for two decades. I asked, "We're doing the right thing, right?" He had experienced a series of frustrations at his job as a real estate broker and seemed ripe for a reinvention as well. "I feel like we're a couple of college kids shipping off on a Eurail for a summer abroad at a youth hostel," I said. Maybe our businesses would be there when we returned, maybe not. At that moment, I couldn't have cared less.

Steve smiled, then reaffirmed our pact to stay "off the office grid." No checking emails. No calls to the office. No exceptions.

THE SABBATICAL

First stop, Barcelona. We wandered the historic El Born neighborhood with its narrow streets and medieval buildings, pausing for midday glasses of rioja and tapas plates of *calamares del campo* and *patatas bravas*. Thoughts of visiting Sagrada Famila or the Picasso Museum evaporated as soon as the waiter suggested a second bottle. On a cafe-lined square, two guitarists played "Hallelujah." Steve and I took it as a sign.

After an afternoon siesta, I panicked. I promised myself I wouldn't even think about work but caved and tried to log on to my office email, only to forget that I had asked staff to change my password. I knew myself too well. I closed the computer before Steve could find me out.

How do I unplug without trying to plug back in every day? Knowing I needed to occupy my mind with something other than work, I started a journal. Decades prior, my sixth-grade teacher, Mrs. Oliver, showed me how to craft one. I've done so ever since.

This new journal would have a special purpose…things I hated about my work. And, to my surprise, the tactic helped free my mind.

Hate list: Not getting any intrinsic or extrinsic rewards. Working hard but not feeling good about it. Business leaders who refused to shoulder any blame for company shortcomings. Slow decision makers. No-decision makers. Pretending to be something we're not. I underlined that last one three times.

Driven by the current e-commerce craze, I'd attempted to change my business from a consulting firm to a software company. I did it for the riches sure to come. But business consulting is highly personalized and hands-on. I foolishly thought I could offer all our services through a program instead of a person. I had no experience in software programming or internet sales. Predictably, the software initiative flopped.

I continued to journal across southern France. But I caved again when I stumbled across an internet café early one morning while Steve slept in. Since I couldn't peek at my office email, I searched for consulting jobs on employment websites. *Ugggh.* I sunk deeper into depression just reading the listings. Low pay, tons of travel, menial tasks. I was not only lost, I was stuck. Every option seemed awful. I bought Steve a coffee and croissant and prayed he wouldn't sense I'd been hacking away on a computer all morning.

Back at our hotel, I picked up my journal and began to browse what I'd penned the days before. I chuckled to myself, realizing something surprising. I missed my clients and the relationships we had forged. Well, most of them, at least. I wondered how they were doing. I realized I would always be invested in their future.

I shifted my list-making to things I liked about my job: seeing entrepreneurs get a product or service off the ground, helping a company rocket up the Inc. 5000 list, showing businesses how to get to scale and reach higher levels of success, counseling leaders on how to fine-tune their purpose or reclaim their weekends...People. I liked the people. They were the heart of my mission, which was to help them create the businesses they always wanted. I got a high out of that. That's my skill, my experience, my purpose. That's my "why"—the answer to why I was in business in the first place.

The companies that embraced our counsel flourished. So why couldn't my own company grow and prosper like the others?

The answer came to me several weeks later in Bellagio. I woke up early and walked out on the hotel balcony overlooking Lake Como. I felt oddly at peace; liberated. A cool fog coated the water like fresh fallen snow. For the last month, through Spain, France, and now Italy, I had tried to analyze why some companies grew and others (including my own) stagnated. *What were the commonalities? What's the secret formula? How do I get some of it?*

Looking out over the serene waters, the words forced their way out of my mouth: "Stop acting like an entrepreneur."

That's it! I wasn't making the type of mature decisions my company demanded in order to grow. I was making decisions based on all the hoopla surrounding entrepreneurship. I'd fallen into the trap of trying to be the next Jeff Bezos,

Arianna Huffington, or worse, any 20-something graduate from an entrepreneurship program who dreams of instant riches.

Stop acting like an entrepreneur. Make the shift from "me" to "we."

Entrepreneurship is essential at the beginning of any business, but it can easily change into a corrosive force. *Why wasn't anyone talking about the other side of entrepreneurship?* I did a Google search of the word. Every article, reference, and mention came encased in glowing positivity: "How to Retire by Age 30!" "Skyrocketing IPOs!" "Work Four Hours a Week!" "All You Need is a Great Idea!"

None of this puffery rang true. I now saw the difference between entrepreneurial success and sustained success and how those forces were often at odds. I'd never made the transition from entrepreneur to collaborative business leader, and my company was paying the price.

I thought about all the businesses I'd worked with over the years and suddenly saw patterns, common sins, and a flawed mentality that linked everything together. I saw the problems clearly. Now I needed to work on the solutions.

Steve took a photo of me. "You just looked so at peace," he said. And he was right. I didn't have all the answers, but I knew the questions to ask. I didn't have it all figured out, but I knew I was on the right path. My nervousness about the future morphed into excitement.

During our last week of the sabbatical, a light-hearted seven days in Tuscany, I crafted a new business plan and toasted with Steve to a new beginning. He thought I was on to something big. So did I.

THE RETURN

Back at home, my staff was less enthusiastic. I told them we were getting rid of half the company's services and nearly all our products. We'd have a new focus, a new mission. In his book *Start with Why*, Simon Sinek counseled the importance of defining why a company is in business. Our company now had a whole new "why." I felt empowered, refreshed, and encouraged.

We began to see the results immediately. Despite the streamlined services, we had more business than we could handle. Every single business measurable—revenue, profit, income, you name it—began to spike. Some staff members loved the new approach. Others quit. But for the first time, we turned away clients. And we fired others who didn't fit our core mission, our why.

My new staff and I spent the next several years doing a deep dive into the qualities of our clients, their industries, and businesses in all fields. We researched approaches, tested ideas, and fine-tuned our programs. They worked beyond expectation.

THE PURPOSE

This book is my quest to share our breakthrough experiences, findings, and proven solutions:

- It's a template for any business or organizational leader interested in avoiding the most common pitfalls of entrepreneurship and a step-by-step guide for how to make the

- crucial shift from a struggling "me" business to a successful "we" business.
- It's for leaders who want to grow startups into thriving companies and for owners of established businesses who want them to grow even more.
- This book is an attempt to debunk the myths surrounding entrepreneurship and romanticized "go-it-alone" business practices and detail the various ways that commonly accepted entrepreneurial approaches are ruining businesses.
- It offers actionable steps toward improving business practices for increased chances of success.

This book focuses on three main concepts: Expose, Educate, and Empower—the motto and mission of my company. Before we jump to the solutions, we first need to better understand the problem and how we arrived there. So, between some of the chapters in the first section of the book, I'll debunk myths and expose disinformation surrounding entrepreneurship.

Next, I'll educate by moving from the macro to the micro using individual stories, case studies, and supporting data to detail the specific ways entrepreneurial practices could be ruining your business. I'll then offer our proven professional strategies for overcoming these common business sins—many of which I committed myself!

Finally, I'll empower readers by giving them the tools and techniques they must possess if they are to evolve from self-absorbed entrepreneurs to successful, collaborative business leaders.

I know many of the stories and much of the information I provide in the coming chapters fly in the face of common perceptions about entrepreneurialism versus collaborative business practices. The media, politicians, universities, and business leaders themselves have created a massive entrepreneurial PR hype machine over decades, and it's going to take a colossal effort to get us back to reality.

This book is my David versus Goliath attempt to do so.

CHAPTER 2

DEATH BY ENTREPRENEURSHIP

On a crisp, spring evening in 2015, more than 100 inventors, consumer product experts, and curiosity seekers gathered in a converted Manhattan warehouse in search of entrepreneurial gold. The event, known as "Eval" (slang for evaluation), took place every Thursday night in the headquarters of Quirky, a much-lauded startup company dedicated to "making invention accessible."

Each Eval followed a similar format. An "invention ambassador" from Quirky would introduce a potential product, then the emcee would open the debate to a panel of experts, the assembled crowd, and viewers who were following the proceedings online. Product debates lasted no more than 10 minutes apiece, after which everyone would vote. A majority approval meant the products would move forward toward development. A thumbs down meant the idea would be cast aside.

With a darkened room, blue backlighting, witty repartee, and even a roving reporter soliciting random "man on the street" opinions from outside the building, Evals had the look and feel of a reality television show—a *Shark Tank*-meets *American Idol* for household gadgets.

And in the center of it all stood Ben Kaufman, master of ceremonies, founder and CEO of Quirky, an entrepreneur's entrepreneur.

Casting directors couldn't have picked a more prototypical character for the role. Kaufman was 28, fast-talking, occasionally foul-mouthed (the unofficial Quirky company motto was "Get Shit Done"), hyper-ambitious, tech-savvy, and well connected. He wore black V-neck Banana Republic T-shirts every day, owning more than 100 of them and explaining that he traveled so much he didn't have time to pack.[1] By the time he was 25, Kaufman had launched several startups considered by many as successful.

No other startup company was as heralded as Quirky. Founded by Kaufman in 2009, Quirky sought to do something unique: crowdsource the invention process. Historically, innovation had been a lonely and often frustrating pursuit. The world was awash in good ideas, but very few inventors were able to develop, distribute, and successfully sell their products on a large scale.

Quirky aimed to change all that. "Send us your best ideas [along with a small fee]," it told inventors. "We will analyze them and vote on them as a community. Then we will pair your inventions with our designers, marketers, and corporate

---

[1] https://www.inc.com/magazine/201310/josh-dean/is-quirky-the-worlds-most-creative-manufacturer.html

partners to shape your products in their best forms possible and bring them to market." The process would be one giant innovation democracy. The best ideas would rise to the top, and anyone who helped along the way would share in the riches to follow.

Inventions and accolades came fast and strong. Kaufman and Quirky developed and brought to market a handful of products from outside inventors that generated modest profits, including a circular power strip called the Power Pivot and a spoon that hung on the side of a coffee cup called MugStir. He raised $6 million, then $16 million, then $68 million, then $79 million from the biggest names in Silicon Valley and the tech world.[2] GE gave him $30 million for an "Internet of Things" subsidiary called Wink, which developed smart home devices.

"Is This the World's Most Creative Manufacturer?" read a headline in *Inc. Magazine*. CBS, ABC, CNN, *Wired*, and *Entrepreneur* showered him with praise. Quirky sold products on the Home Shopping Network, and The Sundance Channel gave Kaufman his own reality TV show. On the global entrepreneurial stage, Ben Kaufman was a megastar.

At Quirky, innovation and speed trumped everything. Evals were designed to showcase that commitment and prove to the world that good ol' American ingenuity was alive and well in the hands of modern-day entrepreneurs.

One evening, Kaufman opened the show with a warm welcome. He quickly explained the process and then exchanged friendly banter with the panel of experts, asking them about current projects. The audience, which included many Quirky

[2] https://www.businessinsider.com/quirky-ben-kaufman-2015-4

employees, sipped wine and drank craft beers in pint glasses with the company logo. The Eval seemed to confirm Glassdoor's high ratings for the firm's fast-paced environment and intelligent staff. Indeed, how many companies allowed employees to vote on every single product in its line? With free drinks, even!

With pleasantries concluded, Kaufman launched into discussing the evening's products for review. On the docket for the night was an auto-replenishing mouthwash dispenser (thumbs down); a similar, automatic replenisher for a candy dispenser (a weak thumbs up, though for "commercial use"); color-changing LED lights for the lawn (thumbs down); pyramid-shaped office lights (thumbs down); an air blaster plugin compressor for air gun toys (thumbs down); Snap Track Wi-Fi Speakers that fit into track lighting (thumbs down); a soundless subwoofer for your pocket or couch, which thumped but didn't emit sound (thumbs down); a children's play perimeter that required kids to wear a bracelet that would sound an alert when the child strayed from an area (thumbs down—"I don't see what's wrong with the leash," opined one panelist); an automatic bed making machine (thumbs maybe); a bike seat that signaled left, right, or stop by projecting images on the biker's back (an enthusiastic thumbs up); and a simple wireless hotplate (thumbs down).

The big winner? The Roller Coaster Engineering Lab, which allowed kids to create their own miniature roller coasters while learning about the laws of physics. Panel members, guests, and people interviewed on the street raved about the offering. They loved the lab's entertainment value and educational component. "Learning when you don't even know you are learning is an amazing thing," said a panelist. "That is like chocolate cake with vitamins in it."[3]

Only one attendee raised a question. He pointed out the display photo was of another, similar product and wondered aloud about competition in the marketplace. "I just want to make sure we are not stepping on someone's toes," he said. The audience and panel quickly green-lighted the product.

Kaufman concluded the Eval by congratulating the participants for their ideas. He also thanked Quirky staffers who worked over the weekend to help with a recall of a home automation hub sold at Home Depot and manufactured by Wink. "Hopefully it goes down in the records as the fastest retail recall in human history," he said. "We were out of retail and back in retail in, like, four days flat."

He ended the evening by promoting the "big Eval next week," which would feature "the conclusion of the incredibly popular Harman Invention Challenge. We got 800 something ideas in headphones!" said Kaufman. "Over the course of the next week, we are going to be working with the Harman team, and we are going to come...with an all-star Eval. The Harman executive team will be there. It is going to be a big show! Until then, continue doing what you do."[4] The audience applauded, and the show wrapped for the week. And...scene.

Kaufman oozed confidence throughout the proceedings. He gave the impression that Quirky had it all—powerful partnerships with companies like GE, Harman, and Mattel; brilliant and hard-working employees; successful products on

---

[3] Quirky (2015, April 23). *Quirky: Live product evaluation.* YouTube. https://www.youtube.com/watch?v=3TTEMnFMkOc.

[4] Quirky (2015, April 23). *Quirky: Live product evaluation.* YouTube. https://www.youtube.com/watch?v=3TTEMnFMkOc.

the market; and a limitless pipeline for new products thanks to a supportive global community of inventors. Big profits awaited anyone involved.

Internally, however, Kaufman knew his world was crumbling. Outsiders were beginning to see it as well. A closer look at the evening's events reveals many of Quirky's lethal problems, starting with Kaufman's mention of the recall.

The home automation hub by Wink was designed to work with a cell phone. Due to an engineering error, the hubs couldn't connect to the internet after a year of use, making the cloud-based product worthless.[5] The glitch followed a series of poor reviews by consumers and tech media.

"To cut to the chase," Wink told users on its website, "we need your Wink Hub back. We'll update it and get it back to you within a few days." Users were encouraged to order pre-paid shipping boxes and offered $50 gift certificates to go toward the purchase of compatible devices.

Quirky/Wink did get the product back on the Home Depot shelves within the week, but larger damage had been done. Thanks to the Wink hub snafu and several other operational issues, investors and potential buyers shied away.[6] GE ended the Wink/Quirky partnership a few months later.[7]

Another problem was that, although the most praised product of the evening was the Roller Coaster Engineering Lab, Kaufman and his panel paid little attention to the audience member who asked about competition. There was

---

[5] https://www.cnet.com/news/quirky-needs-your-wink-hub-back-after-a-security-update/

[6] http://fortune.com/2015/06/12/quirky-wink-funding-products/

[7] https://www.wsj.com/articles/ge-says-quirky-has-hurt-its-reputation-1449179311

competition, and it was significant. K'NEX®, the category leader in build-it-yourself miniature roller coasters, had been successfully selling similar products for years. The photograph Quirky used at the Eval featured a K'NEX coaster. Had a Quirky staffer simply Googled "miniature roller coasters," they would've found K'NEX roller coasters featured on various news outlets. They would've also seen dozens of home videos of elaborate roller coaster creations posted on YouTube.

Kaufman and Quirky committed many of the common entrepreneurial sins I'll be detailing in this book. Instead of settling on a product or two and perfecting them, the company "chased sexy." And chased and chased and chased. They wanted to make 50 new products a year! But not one was essential. Do we really need auto-replenishing candy dispensers or spoons that clip on a coffee cup?

The Quirky devices that did make it to market received a lukewarm reception at best. Customers complained, but there were few revisions. Quirky employees weren't focused on revisions. They spent the bulk of their energy pursuing The Next Big Thing.

As a result, the products felt like a bunch of half-baked, poorly executed ideas spread across 26 product categories. Together, they didn't combine to form a cohesive brand. Most Quirky products sold for low prices, in highly competitive markets, with little markup. In the end, very few turned a significant profit. "For example, the company spent nearly $400,000 developing a Bluetooth speaker that only sold 28 units."[8]

---

[8] https://www.businessinsider.com/quirky-funding-and-changes-2015-6

Kaufman faced problems internally as well—problems common to companies that operate too much like an entrepreneurial startup. It's clear that during the Eval he had a limited grasp of what his engineers and designers were doing during the day. By his own admission, he traveled constantly, usually in search of more funding. A cursory look at Quirky's Glassdoor ratings revealed many seeds of discontent among staff, with Quirky and Kaufman being criticized for poor decision-making, poorly thought-out products, and lack of structure to address problems.

Running low on cash, Quirky began a series of layoffs while closing its satellite offices in Schenectady, Hong Kong, and San Francisco. Top executives, including chief technology officer Steven Heintz, left the company for more stable employment. Internet chatter about the company's demise grew through the well-connected virtual community it had created.

Kaufman continued with the Evals, though by summer he adopted a more somber tone and outlook. Following a series of interviews and appearances during which he talked openly about the cash problems at Quirky, Kaufman sought to reassure growing concerns among the inventor community. At the end of the July 16th Eval, he assured the Quirky community they'd be paid for their efforts, talked about cost-cutting measures, continued to champion the idea behind Quirky, and dismissed an online question about his "exit strategy." "I don't plan on exiting anything," he said. "I am perfectly happy here."

Two weeks later, he resigned. "In light of our ongoing strategy to focus our efforts on Wink, our founder, Ben Kaufman, will no longer serve as the CEO of Quirky," read an announcement from the company. "Left both companies," added Kaufman via Twitter. "Everyone is in good hands."

By the end of September 2015, having burned through more than $175 million in funding with little to show for it, Quirky filed for bankruptcy.[9] It sold the Wink subsidiary for $15 million to Flextronics (later Flex), the company's largest creditor. Quirky had asked for more than twice that amount a few months earlier. Though its devices remain in Home Depot and other retailers, Wink has yet to turn a profit and now faces increasing competition in the smart home device market from giants such as Amazon, Apple®, and Samsung.

The rest of Quirky was sold to a company called Q Holdings for $4.7 million, despite protests from GE that claimed Quirky "caused substantial damage to the reputation of GE and to its trademark."[10]

The new owners relaunched Quirky as a simple online platform for invention collaboration as well as an online shop for its previously developed products. There would be no more large staffs or in-house development, no more big-name collaborations, no more Evals.

Kaufman put some spin on the crash, blaming "the traditional bounds of brick-and-mortar retail."[11] He vanished from the headlines...then quickly reinvented himself with several new ventures, including efforts to sell emoji-themed pool floats and candles he claimed to be scented like states (Homesick Candles).

---

[9] http://fortune.com/2015/09/22/quirky-files-bankruptcy/

[10] https://www.wsj.com/articles/ge-says-quirky-has-hurt-its-reputation-1449179311

[11] http://fortune.com/2016/11/21/buzzfeed-commerce-ben-kaufman/

Meanwhile, the same media outlets that had fueled Quirky's rise to fame now had to admit they were wrong. They did so begrudgingly, if at all.

"Despite an enticing business model and an enthusiastic user community, Quirky faces considerable challenges in reorganizing through its bankruptcy," concluded Fast Company.[12] CNBC, which had named Quirky to its Disruptor 50 list earlier in the year, stressed the company "generated more than $100 million in revenue in 2014" and that Wink products wouldn't be impacted.

Inc. Magazine seemed particularly reluctant. "Before everything fell apart, much worked well at Quirky," concluded senior writer Christine Lagorio-Chafkin.[13] "When all cylinders were firing, the company's website would receive thousands of invention ideas a week, from more than half-a-million users. And each week, it would approve a handful of those products for development—and send a handful of completed products to its retail partners for sale. Strong partnerships—with online shops such as Amazon, posh locales such as the Museum of Modern Art, and big-box stores such as Bed Bath & Beyond, Best Buy, and Target—abounded. And their ranks were growing."

Few questioned the basic business model. And no publication asked the bigger, more important question: is too much entrepreneurship a bad thing? In many people's eyes, a company could never be too innovative or cutting edge.

[12] https://www.fastcompany.com/3051418/quirky-files-for-bankruptcy-agrees-to-sell-smart-home-subsidiary-wink?cid=search

[13] https://www.inc.com/christine-lagorio/jim-collins-steve-jobs-apple-what-i-know-podcast.html

Entrepreneurship is what grabbed the public's attention, piqued the interest of investors, and sold magazines and television ads. Media outlets shook their heads and moved on to other "hot" entrepreneurial startups. They turned the page and continued to fuel the myth.

Unchecked entrepreneurship killed Quirky. An unrealistic view of entrepreneurship killed Quirky. A community of hundreds of entrepreneurs wanting to operate only like entrepreneurs killed Quirky. The company did everything possible to avoid taking that crucial step from a startup mindset to a collaborative leadership approach. Quirky's execution wasn't its biggest problem. It was the entire model.

Unfortunately, this isn't an isolated incident. It's a scenario being repeated daily. Entrepreneurship may be a media darling, but it's also a leading business killer. Bar none.

Hear me out.

Companies large and small hire my business, Collaboration LLC, to help them grow their businesses. The most common problem we see is businesses that start with a good idea, have a little success, then have a hard time translating that early success into a long-term, highly profitable operation. It's like a politician who does a good job getting elected but struggles to govern once in office.

Starting a company and growing a company are two entirely different things. In fact, being a successful business leader and being a successful entrepreneur usually conflict with each other.

When I tell a client they're acting too much like an entrepreneur, they usually balk at the idea at first. "Too much like an entrepreneur?" they say. "I thought that was a good thing. I thought you were either innovating or you were dying."

Entrepreneurship can be an important spark for a new business or a new product, I tell them. But if you continue to operate like a startup, your business will stall and fail. Early success does not always translate into sustained success.

So forget about everything you've heard or read about entrepreneurship, I counsel. Forget about "me," and start thinking about "we." It's a matter of life and death for every company.

The following chapters will show you how to make this all-important shift.

Visit Collaboration-LLC.com for a whitepaper and webinar titled, "Three Pitfalls of an Entrepreneur That Kill Your Business."

CHAPTER 3

LEGGO MY EGO

I can tell within five minutes whether a business leader's ego is going to kill a company. You can too. There's a quiz at the end of this chapter. Take it. Then have your employees take it as well. Tally the results and see for yourself whether your ego provides your company with a healthy dose of confidence or is a serious threat to your business.

With so much puffery and flattery over the last few decades, is it any surprise that today's stereotypical entrepreneurs are a bit full of themselves? At first glance, many of them deserve the plaudits.

Take John Rampton, founder and CEO of Due, an online payment processing company. In college, Rampton earned extra money on the weekends working at a construction site. One day, a large skid steer ran over his leg, snapping it in half. After several surgeries, the doctors told him he would probably never walk again. Rampton refused to give up. He opted for a procedure that included animal stem cell injections. "I've always laughed that I am two-percent lamb in my body because my leg is made out of stem cells from a lamb," said Rampton.[14]

Rampton couldn't walk or leave his bed. But instead of moping, he got to work. He grabbed a laptop and began exploring potential business opportunities. He learned about online marketing and sometimes spent 16 to 20 hours a day researching. More than a year later, he willed himself to walk again after strengthening his legs in a swimming pool. He also started a company that helped real estate agents sell property online, then sold it for eight-plus figures. Healthy and wealthy, he thought he could do anything. A marriage further boosted his spirits and made for a perfect All-American entrepreneur story.

"I made millions of dollars and I went to purchase another company," he said. "Six months later, I went out of business and I lost every penny that I had."

The reason, Rampton explains, was simple: ego. "I started a new venture and acted like I was 'the bomb' and nothing could stop me. This destroyed my business. It wasn't the company, product or people behind the business...it was 100% me that killed this company. As a result, I lost almost everything I owned."[15]

The business he purchased was an e-commerce company called Organize.com, an online competitor to The Container Store®. It sold products primarily through Amazon, shipping from a massive Southern California warehouse with "about

---

[14] https://brand24.com/blog/failure-epic-part-success-john-rampton/
[15] https://www.entrepreneur.com/article/278901#

56,000 skews."[16] Rampton thought he could instantly triple sales by eliminating inefficiencies and boosting the online sales conversion rate.

Amazon requires companies to meet a long list of criteria to sell products on its website. It sets set rigorous standards for quality, honesty, delivery, and customer support. When companies fall behind on any of these fronts, Amazon bars them temporarily. When they fall behind repeatedly, companies receive a letter from Amazon telling them they were banned for good.

That's what happened to Rampton and Organize.com. Rampton ignored warning signs and advice from his coworkers, allowing his ego to guide decisions. "My ego was telling me, 'You are so incredible, you've already thought of and done everything that must be done, period.' Because of this, my ego prevented me from seizing innovative and beneficial opportunities that could've helped my business move forward and succeed."[17]

Many of Rampton's products sold well. Too well. The company quickly ran out of stock on several items, but it continued to sell them. Amazon frowns on this. The practice drives up delivery times and drives down customer satisfaction. Rampton dismissed the warnings, focusing instead on the sales numbers. He acted like he knew better than the mighty e-tailer.

He should've listened to Amazon's warnings and read its requirements a little closer, because as soon as Organize. com's customer satisfaction ratings dipped below Amazon's

---

[16] https://mywifequitherjob.com/john-rampton-amazon-banned/
[17] https://mywifequitherjob.com/john-rampton-amazon-banned/

set standards, the company was thrown off the powerful website for good. This was doubly bad since Rampton had made the bullheaded decision to sell primarily through Amazon instead of selling through a variety of other e-commerce retailers such as Overstock or eBay.

When he received the cease-and-desist letter from Amazon, Rampton knew his company was done. "I have an 80,000,000 square foot warehouse with $150,000 in inventory and $2 million in bills," he told the "My Wife Quit Her Job" podcast. "I ended up selling everything, paid as many bills as I could and then fully left the company, then literally I folded the company and I packed everything in my house, I sold everything; we (he and his wife) moved in our car and we moved home."[18]

Rampton estimated his net worth to be $15 million at the time he purchased Organize.com. Now, thanks to his ego, he had nothing.

Rampton's story is common and age-old. The history books of business are littered with failures that could've been prevented with a little less self-importance and a little more honesty and openness.

Alexander Graham Bell tried to sell the patent for his telephone to Western Union for $100,000. "Mr. Bell," replied Western Union President William Orton, "after careful consideration of your invention, while it is a very interesting novelty, we have come to the conclusion it has no commercial possibilities...What use could this company have for an

---

[18] https://mywifequitherjob.com/john-rampton-amazon-banned/

electrical toy?"[19] You can almost hear the passive-aggressive condescension in his voice.

Kodak pioneered digital photography in the early 1970s but company leaders kept the technology bottled up because they didn't want to hurt their film business. They refused to believe their consumers would prefer to shoot and look at photos on a screen.

Blockbuster had a chance to purchase startup Netflix™ for $50 million.[20] Blockbuster executives laughed at the offer.

Search engine Excite had the opportunity to purchase Google for just $750,000![21] They passed and are now the answer to the trivia question, "What's the worst business decision of the last century"?

Dig into these actions a bit more and you'll see they were all more ego-driven than business-driven. In 2000, at the time of the Netflix offer, Blockbuster reigned as the undisputed leader in video rentals. Netflix had only been around for a couple of years but was already making headway by offering a DVD-by-mail service with one low monthly fee, unlimited usage, and no late fees or shipping fees. You don't have to have an MBA degree to know that cheaper and easier things almost always prevail in the business world.

Blockbuster executives certainly knew the Netflix model had advantages over their expensive brick-and-mortar stores

---

[19] https://www.forbes.com/sites/erikaandersen/2013/10/04/it-seemed-like-a-good-idea-at-the-time-7-of-the-worst-business-decisions-ever-made/

[20] https://variety.com/2013/biz/news/epic-fail-how-blockbuster-could-have-owned-netflix-1200823443/

[21] http://fortune.com/2010/09/29/excite-passed-up-buying-google-for-750000-in-1999/

and expensive late fees. They knew more changes were coming in the ever-changing industry. They saw where the technology was headed. At the very least, they could've purchased Netflix and explored ways to improve their operations as the technology advanced. Instead, they let hubris cloud their judgment. They scoffed at Netflix CEO Reed Hastings and his offer.[22] Blockbuster filed for bankruptcy in 2010. There's only one Blockbuster store remaining in America, an outlet in Bend, Oregon.[23] In early 2019, Netflix boasted a market capitalization of $125 billion.[24]

Sure, it's easy to play Monday morning quarterback with some of these business decisions. We all would've purchased Netflix and Google and Graham's telephone patent, right? I'm not so sure. We're all humans, after all. We're all susceptible to the sneaky, strong forces of pride and arrogance. In our personal lives, that can be a turnoff. In our businesses, it can be a killer.

Take something as basic as a company name, for example. In the late 1970s and early 1980s, as consumers increasingly embraced a variety of diet foods, the Dep Corporation had a bestselling candy that claimed to suppress appetites. The low-calorie chocolates and caramels were perfectly positioned to flourish alongside products such as Diet Pepsi™, Miller Lite®, and I Can't Believe It's Not Butter®. The company enjoyed robust sales...until a public health crisis began

---

[22] http://variety.com/2013/biz/news/epic-fail-how-blockbuster-could-have-owned-netflix-1200823443/

[23] https://www.cnn.com/2018/07/13/us/last-blockbuster-america-trnd/index.html

[24] https://www.thestreet.com/technology/netflix-good-growth-story-despite-turbulence-14824501

to devastate the American LGBTQ+ community in the mid-1980s. The candies, you see, went by the name Ayds.

The obvious and logical choice would've been to change the name. No one in their right mind would sell a product called Cholera or *E. Coli*. But Ayds executives loved their name. They wouldn't budge. They convinced themselves that consumers would be able to differentiate between Ayds and AIDS. Predictably, sales plummeted as the AIDS crisis worsened. After seeing their revenues cut in half, Ayds executives finally decided to change the name in 1988...to Diet Ayds. The products vanished from stores shortly thereafter.

You can see an ego decision from miles away. Literally. It can be a big ol' company name on the side of a fancy new building. Or perhaps it's the naming rights to a professional sports stadium or a college football bowl game. (By the way, is there really a business advantage to the Bad Boy Mowers Gasparilla Bowl or the NOVA Home Loans Arizona Bowl?) An ego decision can be using that private G4 airplane when commercial flights would suffice, or it can be investing in expensive television advertising campaigns that feature the CEO regurgitating platitudes about the company all in the name of "brand recognition."

Whenever I step into a business for the first time, large or small, I take a good hard look at things like the office furniture, artwork on the walls, and computer equipment. Are these items there to impress visitors or help the company perform? I look at the decor and decorations. Are the walls filled with photos of the CEO standing with politicians and celebrities or of company and community gatherings? I take a peek at the parking lot. What kind of a car is the leader driving? Maybe the company is struggling, yet the CEO is parking his new Tesla Model S in front for all to see. Bottom line: I want to know if this is a "me" company or a "we" company.

"Me" companies tend to hire mini-me's—carbon copies of the boss. If bosses are hyper-aggressive and confrontational, you'll see an office full of fighters. If the CEO is a graduate of, say, USC or the University of Texas, you'll behold staffs full of Trojans or Longhorns. I see plenty of offices where employees even mirror their boss's dress preferences, opting for Brooks Brothers shirts or Ferragamo™ pumps. Strong leaders are secure enough to shun a staff of "yes men" and hire a diverse group, one that offers a wide variety of experiences and opinions.

I also like to sit in on company meetings to get a better sense of the culture. Do the CEOs do most of the talking? Do they cut short suggestions from others, or does it feel like a healthy give-and-take? When executives are off base about a topic, do others call them on it? Do the leaders encourage healthy debate? Overall, what's the vibe in the room? Strained? Risk averse? The most important qualities I look for are collaborative discourse and a good dose of humor. Disagreements are great...as long as they're positively framed and good-natured.

Ego-driven CEOs often create companies that are quick to blame others for their lack of success (e.g., it's the economy's fault, there were problems with the supplier in China, it was the bad weather). If the CEO immediately points fingers, the employees will too. "Me-first" leaders also tend to come to meetings underprepared. They shoot from the hip, not caring if that contradicts the hard work of others. They pontificate about a topic, then leave it to others to clean up the mess.

Lack of decision can also be an ego decision. Richard Branson talked about walking into Tower Records decades ago and being blown away. He strolled into the same store years later and saw little to no change. That's when he decided to open a direct competitor, Virgin Megastores. Tower later filed for bankruptcy. The irony is that Branson's stores suffered the same fate after refusing to adapt to changing consumer tastes and music delivery methods. A once global brand is now limited to a couple dozen stores in the Arab world.

Want to know what stocks to short? Walk around a professional sports stadium and write down the company names outside the most expensive suites. Now take a look at their business operations. Has that company grown and evolved significantly over the past few years or is it coasting on its laurels? My guess is the latter.

Look around any city in America today. You'll find business leaders who have had good ideas, worked hard, experienced a little success early on, enjoyed a flattering media portrayal or two, and decided they're the business equivalent to Midas. Everything they touch turns to gold.

But talk to the people around them and you'll hear a different story. Employees complain about micromanagement, unreasonable expectations, or impossible goals. They talk about business leaders who rarely listen, almost never change their minds, or continue arguments just to "win" even if the rest of the company believes they're wrong. Coworkers feel like they can never do enough to prove their worth, to be a true collaborative partner. It's as though there are two companies operating at once—one run by employees and another operating exclusively in the business leader's head.

Steve Jobs was the embodiment of this problem. During his first go-around at Apple, his ego was so out of control that he was fired by the company he cofounded. Apple CEO John Sculley called him a "petulant brat."[25] While his Macintosh division missed its sales target by 90 percent, Jobs obsessed over things like making sure the computers were all a certain color and ignoring warnings that painting the machines made them break down more frequently. He listened to no one.

In his second stint at Apple, Jobs, while still hyper-opinionated and prickly at times, was much more collaborative. In *Becoming Steve Jobs*, authors Brent Schlender and Rick Tetzeli argue that a key to Jobs' success was his ability to mature as both a person and a business leader. As a result, Jobs became a better delegator, manager, and listener.[26]

The authors cite Jobs' willingness to temper his enthusiasm for iMovie® after his colleagues made a compelling case that iTunes® and iPod® would be more lucrative and worthy of the company's support. They were right, and Jobs was wise to heed their advice.

Pixar leaders Ed Catmull and John Lasseter witnessed Jobs' evolution firsthand while Jobs was the majority shareholder of the animation company. "Watching our collaboration, seeing us make ourselves better by working together, I think that fueled Steve," said Lasseter in *Becoming Steve Jobs*. "I think that was one of the key changes when he went back to Apple. He was more open to the talent of others."

---

[25] Isaacson, The Innovators, PAGE NUMBER.
[26] https://www.wired.com/2015/03/steve-jobs-tamed-explosive-genius/

Bestselling author Jim Collins (*Good to Great*) summed up Steve Jobs' evolution succinctly: "He's not a success story. He's a growth story."[27]

THE A-LIST CHECKLIST

OK business leaders, time to get real. You've had a great idea or an innovation that has taken flight in the marketplace. You've worked hard to build your company from scratch and have tasted some success. Congratulations. Here's a pat on the back.

Now forget about all that. Put the awards in a drawer. Don't let your past success color reality. Know there is a big difference between early success and sustainable success. So focus on the future. You're in a new phase now. Time to shift from "me" to "we."

Think of it like campaigning versus governing. You've won the election. In many ways, the election was a referendum on you and your ideas. Great. You won a popularity contest. Now it's time to manage and lead. And you can't lead through stump speeches. You need to become a collaborative leader. You need to delegate and cede responsibility. It's not about you anymore.

Your ego might've helped get your company off the ground. Now it's something that can run your company into the ground.

How do you prevent your ego from sabotaging your business? Time for what I call the A-List Checklist.

---

[27] https://www.inc.com/christine-lagorio/jim-collins-steve-jobs-apple-what-i-know-podcast.html

Acknowledge

This is by far the hardest step: acknowledging that your ego may sometimes limit your company's growth and potential. Many business leaders don't see the problem until their business has crashed and burned. Wiser business leaders ask themselves tough questions at every stage. Do I know enough and have enough experience to navigate this company properly? Am I blazing a path on my own, or am I navigating in conjunction with my team?

The strongest leaders are the ones who see their weaknesses, then quickly confess them to themselves and their teams. I can't begin to tell you how refreshing it is to hear a CEO say something like, "I don't have all the answers." Good leaders listen more than talk.

John Rampton realized he had an ego problem after the collapse of Organize.com. Before he moved on to his next business venture, he accepted the fact his personality was a key contributor to the failure. He vowed to make changes. This is crucial. If you don't admit you have a problem, you can never move on to problem-solving.

Assess

I've yet to meet a business leader who feels the company can't do any better. Well, growth requires honesty. And plenty of it. Time for a brutally frank assessment of your talents and shortcomings. Maybe you're a great salesperson but are horrible with numbers. Maybe you love managing people but feel insecure about your grasp of technology. Solicit the opinion of others and take their input seriously. Try to avoid the "yes men." Reaching out to an outside consultant can be helpful in assessing the skills needed at every level of the company and determining where the firm is coming up short.

Rampton's assessment was candid and hugely beneficial for any future project he pursued. He concluded that he didn't think he had to learn or change his management while running Organize.com. He had ignored possibilities and overestimated his abilities. He micromanaged, and he didn't ask for help. He made every decision about himself. He always had to "win" in his exchanges with his employees. That's exactly the type of strong self-appraisal needed for success.

Ask an Advisor

Maybe you already have a mentor or two. If not, you should seek one out immediately. The quickest and easiest way to keep an ego in check is by consulting a professional who can call you on your BS, share stories of similar missteps, and help you overcome challenges. Look around. There are probably many people you could consult with on a formal or informal basis. Based on my client experiences and work with leadership groups, I'm certain most would be honored to help. You just have to ask.

If that fails, consider hiring a professional consultant. Ask around to see if any fellow business leaders have had a positive experience with a particular consultant or firm. Be specific on what you want from them and try to hire an individual or company with precisely the type of experience you need.

After a survey of more than 200 CEOs and high-ranking executives, Stanford Graduate School of Business reported that nearly all the respondents claimed they enjoyed and valued advice from mentors and coaches, yet only one-third regularly sought outside leadership advice.[28] What's one big thing holding them back? Ego.

When deciding on his next step, John Rampton turned to someone he trusted. "Jobs had Wozniak. Gates had Allen," wrote Rampton in *Entrepreneur*.[29] "My billionaire mentor, Phil, showed me what my ego wouldn't let me see, that without these people companies like Apple and Microsoft™ wouldn't have grown into the juggernauts they are today."

Action Plan

So you've completed your assessment, copped to some tough truths about your leadership style, and sought advice from a mentor. I'd say you're far ahead of the pack, but I don't want to refuel that ego!

Now it's time to put everything into practice. An action plan is essential whether you're starting a new business or re-energizing a current one. Spell out in detail exactly how you're going to conquer the obstacles that have stalled prior efforts.

Set goals but make them realistic. Entrepreneurs tend to overshoot when they start a business. They talk about franchising immediately or toppling an industry giant. If you have a sky-high goal, great. The trick is to reveal that goal to others gradually. Don't overwhelm colleagues and customers right away. Imagine those recent college graduates who join

---

[28] https://www.gsb.stanford.edu/faculty-research/publications/2013-executive-coaching-survey

[29] https://www.entrepreneur.com/article/278901#

your company. They're just trying to master the basics, and you're spouting off about "disrupting" an industry. You'll end up paralyzing the poor souls. Easy, tiger. Your company will be much better in the long run if you make the goals attainable and easy to understand by all. Simon Sinek refers to this as the "infinite game" which focuses on resilience to thrive in an ever changing world

A good action plan also includes a better definition of your role. Most entrepreneurs are awful at this. They tend to see their role as everything. And too often they end up doing a little bit of everything poorly.

Use this advice: fewer roles, better roles. Limit your role to your top skills and areas where you can help the most. For everything else, trust and delegate. It's hard as hell for many entrepreneurs to cede control of parts of their company operations. It's also essential if they ever wish for that company to grow and prosper.

At the same time, strive to attain new skills or knowledge. If you've done a thorough job assessing your impact on the company, it's time to polish up those areas that could use a little work. Take a course to improve your computer skills, for example. Better yet, arrange to have your technology person give you a few tutorials. You'll gain a skill, empower an employee, and build collaboration in the process.

Here's a way to trick your ego: See shortcomings not as a weakness but as challenges. Dare your ego to learn a foreign language, design a website, or better understand a new industry. Use specific benchmarks to keep the challenge alive and measurable. A healthy ego hates to lose. Why not use a little mental judo here and turn that force into a win?

Apologize

If you've done an honest self-assessment, you'll likely find instances where you have been wrong and others have been right. It's time to tell them you're sorry for ignoring their suggestions. Go talk to the marketing person who advocated for social media or the customer who pleaded with you to offer online discounts. Look, they aren't always going to be right, but you want them to work with you not against you. Tell them you'll try harder to listen in the future. You'll buy yourself a world of goodwill.

■ ⟶ ■

After the failure of his business, John Rampton took all the steps on this A-List. He assessed his shortcomings as a business leader and the structural flaws in his old company. Then he took actionable steps to overcome those challenges. Did he lose his ego completely? Of course not. But he took steps to keep it in check. He realized the damage an unrestrained ego can cause any business, new or established.

In 2015, licking his wounds and working to prevent new ones, Rampton purchased an online invoicing and payments company called Due as mentioned earlier. After having experienced cash flow problems firsthand, he was now helping small business owners speed up and improve their cash flow. He hired a talented staff and let them do their jobs. He also rebranded the company and started offering helpful content for free, including his own blog as well as regular articles he pens for *Inc.*, *Entrepreneur*, and *Time*. The multimillion-dollar company quickly doubled in size. Ego altered.

LEGGO MY EGO

PUT YOUR EGO TO THE TEST

Score one point for every "yes" answer. If your final tally is 1–3, congratulations, your ego is in check. If your score totals 4–6, beware, possible danger ahead. If your score total is 7 or higher, your business is in danger of being destroyed by a super-sized ego.

10 Questions for Business Leaders

1. Is this company *the* major part of my identity?

2. Do I have photos of myself with celebrities, politicians, and famous people on my walls and desk?

3. When disagreements or setbacks happen, is it hard not to take things personally?

4. Does anyone else care about this company as much as I do?

5. Am I usually the most knowledgeable person in the room?

6. Is loyalty more important to me than experience or skill?

7. If I left, would this company fold?

8. When problems happen, is someone else usually at fault?

9. Do I tend to ignore advice if it conflicts with my views?

10. Is trial and error the best way for this company to grow?

47

10 Questions for Employees

1. Does my boss usually talk down to me?

2. Do I wish my boss would quit micromanaging and just let me do my job?

3. Does my boss tend to turn discussions into win-lose arguments?

4. Is it rare that my boss takes the blame for something?

5. Does my boss know what's really going on at this company?

6. Does my boss know much about my life outside of work?

7. Does this company care more about image than results?

8. Does my boss take things too personally?

9. Does my boss seem to change goals and strategies without input?

10. Does my boss tend to ignore feedback that conflicts with his/her views?

SUMMARY POINTS

- The unchecked ego is a frequent and widespread business killer. It can prevent you from seeing your companies and competition honestly and objectively, which can lead to foolhardy decisions and disgruntled staff. The problem is especially prevalent among new business leaders who have experienced a little success early in their careers.
- The first steps to keeping an ego in check are to acknowledge it, assess it, and identify where it's having an impact. Mentors, advisors, and coaches can help you realize when your ego is impeding progress and show you how to overcome challenges.
- Next, craft an action plan—one that includes realistic goals and clearly defined roles—to help ensure your ego doesn't wreak havoc going forward. Then make sure to apologize to anyone you may have offended in the past.

Visit Collaboration-LLC.com for a downloadable "Put Your Ego to The Test" quiz.

CHAPTER 4

CHASING SEXY

$\mathbf{D}$id you hear about Elon Musk?

He's selling flamethrowers on Twitter! It's to support his Boring Company, and he plans to drill a network of underground tunnels to ease traffic congestion.[30] He's trying to privatize space travel, launch 7,000 low-orbit satellites for a global internet system,[31] and colonize Mars with his SpaceX corporation. He does that while serving as the CEO of Tesla Motors, the electric car maker that hopes to overtake the automobile industry in the near future. Musk and Tesla also purchased SolarCity Corp., a renewable energy company Musk helped found with his cousins, Lyndon and Peter Rive.[32]

[30] http://money.cnn.com/2018/02/01/technology/flamethrower-elon-musk-boring-company-sold-out/index.html

[31] http://fortune.com/2018/02/22/spacex-starlink-satellite-broadband/

[32] https://www.biography.com/people/elon-musk-20837159

Meanwhile, Musk announced plans for a "hyperloop," an invention to transport people through tubes in pods that will reach speeds of 700 miles per hour. He also offered to build a high-speed loop between downtown Chicago and O'Hare International Airport. He's backing an effort to create devices that can be implanted in the brain to allow humans to better interact with computers. And, oh by the way, he initially made his money as the cofounder of PayPal®.

I love reading about Musk. He's larger than life, a thrillionaire, as they say, a super wealthy entrepreneur trying to turn science fiction into reality. He's the real-life Iron Man. Literally. Robert Downey credits Musk as the inspiration for his performance of Tony Stark in the Iron Man movie series.[33]

Musk seems like a decent man to boot—starting educational foundations, parenting five children, pledging to give the bulk of his $20 billion fortune to charity. I'm inspired by Musk and entertained by him…I just won't ever invest in his companies.

Why not? His initiatives are bold, headline-grabbing, and entrepreneurial to the core. But dig beyond the headlines and you'll see that they aren't hugely profitable. Let's take another look at the accomplishments listed at the beginning of the chapter.

After losses of more than $776 million in 2016 and $2 billion in 2017,[34] Tesla reported its first profitable quarter in late 2018.[35] I'm far from convinced they'll stay that way.

---

[33] http://www.todayifoundout.com/index.php/2011/08/robert-downey-jr-modeled-his-portrayal-of-tony-stark-after-elon-musk-one-of-the-founders-of-zip2-paypal-tesla-motors-and-spacex/

[34] https://www.theverge.com/2018/2/7/16986396/tesla-2017-full-year-earnings-model-3-production

[35] https://www.cnn.com/2018/10/26/tech/tesla-profit/index.html

From day one, the company has over-promised and under-delivered, struggling with production snags, quality control, and cash flow.

Musk needs to iron out those problems quickly, because a host of competitors are diving into the high-end electric vehicle market, including Jaguar, Porsche, Audi, and BMW.[36] On the other side of the price spectrum, Ford, Hyundai, Kia, and Nissan are all selling less expensive competitor models with plans for more. Toyota announced it will offer an electric version for all its models by the year 2025.[37]

Sure looks like Tesla is getting squeezed on both ends. My money's on the established automakers who have much better production, service, and distribution networks. Wall Street seems wary as well. "You have to ask yourself what will happen first: that Elon Musk will fly to Mars with SpaceX, or that he will finally operate Tesla in the black," joked one analyst.[38] "We consider it a big mistake that Tesla and Elon Musk do not concentrate on a few important things, but instead appear to do everything a little bit, but nothing all the way through." Bingo.

Musk labeled the Tesla-SolarCity merger a "no-brainer." Maybe that means he didn't use his brain during that transaction. SolarCity stock hit a high of $86 in early 2014. Saddled with ballooning debt, stagnating sales, and decreasing government subsidy programs for solar customers, the

[36] https://www.theverge.com/2018/3/10/17096608/tesla-jaguar-porsche-audi-evs-geneva-motor-show-2018

[37] https://www.usatoday.com/story/money/energy/2017/12/23/electric-vehicles-toyota-could-become-teslas-next-big-headache/977877001/

[38] https://www.cnbc.com/2017/11/28/analyst-jokes-musk-will-make-it-to-mars-before-tesla-is-profitable.html

company's fortunes took a nosedive over the next several years, dipping to under $20 a share. That's when Musk and Tesla purchased the company for $2.6 billion in an all-stock deal.[39] Together, the companies would provide eco-minded consumers with one-stop shopping, he preached. Why just purchase a new Tesla ($36,000–$250,000)[40] when you can also buy Tesla residential solar panels ($50,000 for an average-sized home) and a Tesla Powerwall battery ($7,000) to store your energy, all from the same showroom?

Some shareholders and watchdogs immediately questioned the move, saying it looked more like a personal and family bailout than a wise business acquisition. Was Musk rescuing one of his failing companies with another?[41] Months after the merger, Lyndon and Peter Rive quit Tesla, leaving their cousin as promoter-in-chief.

Musk promotes SpaceX™ as an up-and-coming rival to aerospace giants such as Boeing, Lockheed Martin, and Airbus. The company has had its ups and downs, experiencing a series of failed launches before a string of successful ones. But even with several lucrative NASA contracts in hand, SpaceX is nowhere near its competitors in terms of revenues and profits.[42] Boeing and Lockheed Martin consistently post annual profit margins of more than 10 percent, while SpaceX operates

---

[39] https://www.washingtonpost.com/news/the-switch/wp/2016/06/22/this-is-why-elon-musk-is-buying-solarcity/

[40] http://money.cnn.com/2017/11/17/technology/tesla-roadster/index.html

[41] https://www.forbes.com/sites/petercohan/2016/06/22/4-reasons-tesla-motorssolarcity-is-a-2-86-billion-anti-no-brainer/#6cd279815fc6

[42] https://www.wsj.com/articles/exclusive-peek-at-spacex-data-shows-loss-in-2015-heavy-expectations-for-nascent-internet-service-1484316455

in the red.[43] Colonizing Mars sounds fantastic. But if I'm a shareholder, I want my company to be far more grounded.

The "hyperloop" high-tech transport to O'Hare and the brain chip initiatives are little more than press releases and Musk charm. The Boring Company (love the name, by the way) is still a nascent enterprise with little more than concepts and dreams to peddle. It has no significant clients or projects at the moment. That's why Musk is selling flamethrowers to generate a little interest and revenue.

I put an asterisk next to flamethrowers because they aren't really flamethrowers at all. They're just propane torches inside toy gun shells. You can produce your own for about $100 and purchase the parts at Walmart. Musk peddled his for $500 and claims to have sold out his allotment of 20,000.[44] This didn't sit well with fire officials who pointed out the obvious hazards of blasting flames indoors or out. Trial lawyers must be lining up court cases already. I think I'll pass on investing in the flamethrowers.

I'm going to pass on anything relating to Musk for the time being. Do the math. How many minutes in each day does he have to dedicate to space travel, to solar power, to electric cars, to hyper-loops, let alone essential things like, say, sleeping? Even if Musk never slept, could he muster the mind power demanded by these Herculean tasks? Of course not.

[43] https://www.fool.com/investing/2017/02/05/how-profitable-is-spacex-really.aspx

[44] Browne, Ryan. "Elon Musk's Boring Company Sells All of Its Flamethrowers in Less than a Week." *CNBC*, CNBC, 1 Feb. 2018, https://www.cnbc.com/2018/02/01/elon-musks-boring-company-sells-all-of-its-flamethrowers.html.

I think there is a little bit of Musk in every entrepreneur. We love the next big idea, the flashy new object, the game-changing breakthroughs ahead. As entrepreneurs, we have brains that are trained to think that way. I call it "chasing sexy." It can be addictive, fun, and applauded by everyone around you. But chasing sexy can also be a killer for your business.

Let's say you meet someone great, sparks fly, and now you want a long, successful relationship. Are you better off focusing on your new partner or constantly glancing around to check out the other options? I cringe when business leaders tell me they're "serial entrepreneurs." People, serial anything is bad—entrepreneurs, daters, husbands, killers, you name it.

And just like the dating scene, it's fine to think about sexy, just don't chase sexy. Let it walk right out the door. Building a successful business takes time and focus.

So forget chasing sexy. Chase steady. You know what I find attractive in a business? Boring. Boring is profitable. I love non-flashy, wisely focused, long-standing businesses that deliver solid results year after year. Boring. I love boring. You can bank on boring.

What's "boring?" Restaurants or food trucks that offer only a few items but make them so well that people line up to get served. I'm thinking about places like a popular taco truck or pizza joint. Or Le Relais de Venise L'Entrecôte, a small restaurant chain in London, Paris, Mexico City, and New York. They sell steak frites, green salad, and wine. Strike that. They sell damn good steak frites, green salad, and wine. That's it. Nothing more. And no substitutions, please.

There's also Café du Monde in New Orleans. They serve beignets ($2.14 for an order of three), coffee, and a couple other nonalcoholic drinks. Their menu is so small it fits on the side of a napkin holder. They spend pennies to make the French doughnuts and coffee, then sell them at a high markup. They're open 24 hours a day, seven days a week, and there's almost always a line out the door.

I love companies that grow in revenue and profit while keeping their offerings laser focused. This can be anything from a local real estate agency that concentrates on a specific part of town to a mid-size insurance company that offers select policies to a national firm with just a handful of products that sell and sell well. I'm talking about such companies as In-N-Out Burger®, Zippo™, WD-40™, Spanx™, or Crocs™. In the tech world, it's businesses such as Dropbox™, YouTube™, Zillow®, or hundreds of other B2B companies that deliver results year after year. They've all turned niches into riches.

Warren Buffet has become one of the world's wealthiest businessmen by targeting his investments to companies he can understand within 10 minutes.[45] His uber-successful Berkshire Hathaway portfolio includes 100 percent holdings in such "boring" companies as Dairy Queen®, Duracell™, GEICO, Fruit of the Loom®, and See's Candies®; as well as minority stakes in American Express®, The Coca-Cola Company, The Kraft Heinz Company, and Apple.[46]

Yes, Apple. Apple fits perfectly into this list. The planet's most attractive innovator doesn't chase sexy. When you walk into an Apple store, you know exactly what you're going to

---

[45] http://www.businessinsider.com/warren-buffett-best-investing-advice-for-beginners-2017-11

[46] https://en.wikipedia.org/wiki/List_of_assets_owned_by_Berkshire_Hathaway

see: a limited number of sleek computers, iPhones®, iPads®, and Apple Watches® all laid out in an attractive, minimalist showroom. You're not going to be confused or surprised by anything, even if the products are new models. That's because Apple made the choice to make a handful of products and make them better than anything else on the market. Boring. Brilliant.

Warren Buffett and Elon Musk are both involved with dozens of business ventures, far more than any CEO can handle alone. The difference is Buffett doesn't pretend to lead everything. To the contrary, he brags about hiring good people, then letting them do their job. Musk remains CEO of his companies and acts as spokesperson. Buffett is focused. Musk is not. Buffett is chasing steady. Musk is chasing sexy.

CHASING STEADY

I wouldn't bet on Elon Musk, but I would bet on Chuck Matthews. His business journey began back in 1986, when, on a trip to Brazil, he noticed a double-headed ceiling fan cooling customers at a neighborhood cafe and juice bar. He liked the design, the way the fan spun and rotated, and how it moved air efficiently throughout the room.

As luck would have it, Matthews was introduced to a local woman whose family business made the fans. She invited him to their small manufacturing facility and his interest grew. "Cool product," he said to himself. "Maybe I'll buy one for myself someday."

"I wasn't thinking anything more than that. Brazil was just coming out of military rule, and the import/export business was tough because of all the government restrictions," says Matthews.[47]

Six years later, he returned to Brazil. The economy had brightened a bit and some of the trade barriers had been removed. Matthews purchased the ceiling fan, brought it back home to Chicago, and installed it in his living room. He received numerous compliments from friends who visited, including words of praise from a woman who worked at a lighting showroom in the city. She offered to sell the fans at her store if Matthews could supply them.

He knew little about the fan business or importing in general. But he knew he liked the fan and decided to take the woman up on her offer. He contacted the Brazilian manufacturer and imported three double-headed ceiling fans. His education began immediately.

"I just showed up to the airport to pick up my fans," he said. "I had no idea about any permits or fees. Luckily, Customs gave me my first-time exemption and I was on my way."

When Matthews opened the boxes, he discovered a mishmash of materials. "The quality wasn't great. Some parts were made of aluminum, so they'd oxidize. Also, component sizes and finishes weren't uniform." He brainstormed about ways to improve the product.

The three fans sold at the Chicago showroom, and Matthews ordered more from Brazil. Then more. And more. And eventually he accumulated 100, which he painstakingly assembled in his basement.

He was encouraged by the initial success, but he knew the products could be better. So, he took a trip across the

[47] https://matthewsfan.com/about-us/

country, visiting lighting showrooms and asking for advice from experts at every stop. "Interchangeable parts, uniform component sizes and finishes, better materials, different colors, set specs—I knew if I wanted the business to grow I would need to make significant improvements to the products." He began to sketch and spec his own designs.

While Matthews tinkered with the fans, he worked a variety of day jobs, including stints as an insurance salesman and as a trader at an ethanol company. Then a big break, one that would allow him to shift his focus to fans full time.

"I was fired!" he said. A severance package from his final employer enabled him to start the Matthews Fan Company.

From that day forward, Matthews has worked to create and sell the highest quality fans on the market. His indoor and outdoor fans are known for their unique designs, top-of-the-line materials, energy efficiency, and optimal performance.

Matthews' insistence on excellence and his laser focus have led his company to grow from a staff of one person to 21, from a single fan design to several dozen, and from a lone showroom to a global network.

That's not to say Matthews hasn't always resisted the temptation to chase sexy. "My father has given me a lot of great business advice over the years. Two pieces of which I wish I had listened to were—never take on a business partner and be careful about moving out of your comfort zone," he said. "I should have listened to him. Instead I took on a partner and started a lighting company."

While his fan business was taking off, when Matthews should've continued his commitment to growing the line, he instead diverted his resources and attention to the new lighting business. The recession of 2007 hit, the partner quit, and both businesses struggled…a lot. "It was the worst decision I ever made."

The success of his fans lifted him from the stumble. Today, Matthews is back in his comfort zone and is there to stay. He's expanded his high-end line and has started a new line, Atlas Fan Company, with models that start at a lower price point. The Matthews Fan Company continues to grow at a steady clip and Matthews is widely recognized as one of the premier fan makers on the planet.

Matthews and business leaders like him understand that "chasing steady" means knowing what you do well, focusing on how you can maximize those markets, and resisting the urge to do anything that will cause you to lose customers and business.

Often, long-standing companies feel the need to chase sexy, especially as the business changes hands to younger generations. New business leaders want to make their imprint. It's great to build on success, crucial even. It's another thing to take the company in an entirely new direction.

STREAMLINING YOUR MISSION AND VALUES

I have collaborated with a family-owned insurance agency that has been in business since the 1800s. Morris & Garritano has been an integral part of the Central Coast of California for as long as anyone can remember. The company provides commercial and personal insurance along with employee benefit services, while helping support growth and prosperity throughout the region. It's the type of business to which nearly everyone in town has a personal connection.

"That family culture is a real sense of pride," said CEO Brendan Morris, who along with his sister, COO Kerry Morris, is a third-generation Morris working for the company. "It's been a big part of our success."

For decades, the business operated in a similar manner to previous generations: client- and employee-focused. But several years ago, the marketplace began to shift between new technology companies entering its space and consolidation of the players within the industry. This applied pressure on Morris to think more strategically about the future of his agency.

In addition, two other factors were impacting the culture and future of Morris & Garritano. First, Brendan and Kerry were now leading a larger organization, not just a small family business that they or previous leaders had managed. And second, the integration of an earlier competitor acquisition was creating challenges within the culture of the organization.

The culture was losing steam for change and employees were becoming disenfranchised. "We realized we had to redefine our future as well as the 'why' we do what we do," said Brendan Morris. "We had all these great people, but if we as leaders couldn't describe our core values or mission, much less the vision for the future, how could we expect our team to be excited about where we work and where we are going?"

Brendan stated, "Kerry and I realized we needed to grow to stay competitive as well as change how we led the organization. We were putting too much pressure on our employees with these missing components. We needed to refocus."

Collaboration LLC organized a series of sessions to help Morris & Garritano regain that focus. The company needed to step back and ask itself some essential, yet frequently ignored, questions: Who are we? Why are we in business? What are we passionate about?

To find the answers, we started with their mission and their values. The mission statement and the list of values had ballooned over the years, a common occurrence with companies that have been around for generations. Different leaders tend to add their two cents. Quick aside: if you have more than a handful of values, you have none. If you can't recite your values by heart, it's time to reevaluate them. Or, as Brendan Morris explained, "If we couldn't name them (our values), we couldn't live them." Great advice.

Through work sessions and with ample time to reflect, Morris & Garritano streamlined its mission and values and then its longer-term vision. This sharpened focus allowed Morris and his team to address culture challenges from the past and provide a renewed sense of purpose and direction for all employees while beginning the process of growing strategically to remain relevant within their industry and marketplace.

SHIFTING FROM CHASING SEXY
TO CHASING STEADY

Take a good look around your company. Are you or others chasing sexy? Grab a piece of paper and write two columns: Sexy and Boring. Now list all your new business efforts over the last year in one column or the other. Which column is longer?

Once your company experiences a bit of success, it's crucial to forget sexy. Instead, do everything possible to build on that success. Dump the spaghetti-on-the-wall way of doing business—pursuing different approaches with the hope that one sticks. The only guarantee with that strategy is a big ol' mess.

I meet with a lot of clients and potential clients who want to chat about the state of their business. One of the first things I notice is when a business leader wants to talk about a new idea or a new venture before they want to discuss the company's current strengths and flaws. It's a red flag. Some CEOs and business leaders seem to change their focus every single time we sit down. I call this the "book-of-the-month club" strategy, one destined for failure. They read a book or an article about a trend or emerging market and want to immediately alter the whole company focus.

That's when I know we have some work to do. Without dampening enthusiasm, I try to get that business leader to shift from outcome to process. "Hey, you might be entirely correct about selling surfboards in China or solar panels to universities, but let my collaboration team and me better define your strengths to increase your chances for success. Before your company jumps into an expensive new venture, let's do a few internal drills." It's a five-step process:

Step 1: Craft an Anti-Mission Statement.
This is a fun and surprisingly productive way to start. Organize a series of meetings or emails to gather thoughts on what the company isn't. Employees love doing this, from the CEO on down. Ask them to include failures from the past, embarrassing situations, or times when the company felt like a fish out of water. Where do we come up short when

competing with other businesses? Why do people tell us no? Honestly, what do we suck at? You'll be surprised by the answers. Very rarely is there clear agreement on everything. Oftentimes bosses see their company as one thing and the employees see it as another. Time to have some discussions and get on the same page.

The anti-mission statement is a good model for getting leaders and entrepreneurs to more frequently use the most important word in business: "no." The business you say "no" to is more important than the business you say "yes" to. Or, as Warren Buffett concluded, "The difference between successful people and really successful people is that really successful people say no to almost everything."[48] An anti-mission statement will help you develop your no's.

Step 2: Craft a Mission Statement.
Creating an anti-mission statement is also a necessary step toward establishing a clear and useful mission statement, one that is as detailed as possible and specifies purpose, values, goals, and markets served. Use conversational English; lose the corporate speak. Any mission statement with words such as "ideation" or "deliverables" or "change agents" isn't a directive to your employees and clients, it's gobbledygook. And it's a signal that you don't have your act together.

---

[48] https://www.forbes.com/sites/sap/2015/08/12/quotes-on-saying-no/#222e33625555

Step 3: Take the Ebenezer Scrooge Test.

So you had some productive fun tossing out everything your company shouldn't be pursuing. Next, you drafted a mission statement summarizing why you're in business, what you offer, and how you serve your customers. Great. Now it's time to test that mission statement with something I call the Ebenezer Scrooge test: evaluate your business's past, present, and future.

Start by evaluating your past. Were your efforts in sync with your current focus? Where and when were you most successful? Do any past successes or failures require you to rethink your mission going forward?

It's fine for a company to start out doing something and then shift to entirely different markets. William Wrigley Jr. began by selling baking powder and soap. Gum was a giveaway, an enticement to get folks to buy his soap. When enough people told him they preferred the gum to the soap, he shifted focus.[49] Tiffany and Co. started out as a stationery company. Taco Bell was originally a hot dog stand.[50] Most people think Warren Buffett founded Berkshire Hathaway. In actuality, the company began in 1839 and operated as a textile manufacturer for more than a century. Buffett purchased it in 1962 and gradually turned it into a holding company. His shareholders have been happy ever since.

---

[49] http://mentalfloss.com/article/22822/15-companies-originally-sold-something-else

[50] https://www.huffingtonpost.com/2014/01/08/weird-business-origins_n_4546213.html

Like Ebenezer Scrooge, these businesses made their pivots after confronting their past. Then they altered their missions accordingly.

After confronting your past, face your present. Assess how your current mission aligns with your business. This is a common source of frustration. I see many companies in which management and employees are pursuing different objectives. The differences might be slight, but if you multiply them throughout the company and over time, the results can be catastrophic.

For example, say you're a restaurant owner in a university town. You started the operation after learning how to cook food from your Tuscan grandmother. She gave you all her recipes. The townspeople love the food and have kept your business open and profitable for a decade. Business is "good, but it can always be better." So you hire a young marketing manager. She hustles to bring in the college crowd with drink specials and happy hour food. The restaurant is more crowded, but the profits don't grow as you hoped. Soon you begin to lose the regulars, and Yelp reviewers complain about the noise and service delays. When the school year ends, you struggle to stay in business during the summer.

This is a common occurrence across all industries—leaders and employees who think they're working toward a common goal (growth, popularity, profit) yet are often pursuing different strategies and objectives. Before you can grow, you need to better define your business, starting with why you opened in the first place. Just like Scrooge, you need to evaluate the present if you want to manage the future.

Finally, once you've aligned the past and present, aim your mission toward the future. Put it to the test. Ask your employees and leaders, "If we continue to do what we do, and do it well, where will we be in a year? Two years? Five? Do we foresee any changes in our markets or client base that will force us to change tactics or expand offerings?"

All companies need a little time to grow into mature, successful businesses. Make sure that time and effort aren't wasted with a snap judgment or trendy choice. Otherwise, you'll find yourself starting from scratch after an untimely death of your business.

Step 4: Put the Mission Statement into Practice.
After the Christmas Carol review of your company's past, present, and future mission, it's time to put the words into action by embedding the focus throughout the organization, starting at the top.

I ask CEOs to give me a copy of their to-do lists. We go through them item by item, repeatedly asking the same question. Does this further the mission? If yes, keep the item on the list. If not, scratch it out. Politely decline. Say no, then pat yourself on the back for saying no.

Have your employees go through the same drill. Talk with them about their jobs and how they spend their days. What can they discard as "chasing sexy?" Where can they best allocate their time and talents? The clearer the mission, the easier the jobs that follow.

Step 5: Put the Mission into Action.
The final step is to make the mission more than words. Make sure it permeates every aspect of your business. How do you do this? Take a quick inventory of all the internal interactions at your company. Is the company mission something hardwired into these functions, or is it lip service? Is it part of hiring, evaluations, performance reviews, meetings, and awards?

Next, look outside the company. Are you giving the same consistent messages to subcontractors and consultants, business partners, customers, the media, and the public at large? Your consultants and partners are just as likely to chase sexy. Are you keeping them focused or allowing them to roam outside your mission? Your advertising firm might have dozens of creative ideas, but how many match your mission? Even investors frequently chase sexy, encouraging business leaders to examine a new market or different approach. If it furthers your mission, great. If not, politely tell them you're trying to maximize growth and profits...for them!

CHASING STEADY IN ACTION

I love it when the mission filters out to every nook and cranny, inside the company and out, from email signatures to the office decor to charitable activity. If you're a software company that services the healthcare industry, I want to see photos of nurses with your products. I want that email sign-off to include a link to the article that proclaimed your firm, "A Top Choice for Health Care Software." I want your mission to come through all your advertising, public relations, sales efforts, and community relations.

As business leaders, we tend to think that employees and customers understand the mission as well as we do. We think we're being repetitive if we stress it frequently. Lose those thoughts. Immediately. Based on my experience, only 10 percent of business leaders know their mission, resist the urge to chase sexy, and communicate the mission sufficiently. And even then, the company is always susceptible to new flirtations with chasing sexy.

Starbucks® is a good example of this. Howard Schultz, former chair and CEO of Starbucks, purchased the six original Starbucks stores along with a roasting plant in 1987. He combined them with his other coffee shops and kept the name Starbucks. His purpose and mission were clear: give customers high quality coffee, including the espresso drinks Schultz enjoyed during trips to Italy. Until then, Americans were fine with Folgers™ and Sanka™. Schultz hooked us on lattes and cappuccinos.

Starbucks expanded with dizzying speed. I love the scene from the movie *Best in Show* in which Parker Posey's character deadpans that she met her husband at a Starbucks. "Not at the same Starbucks, but we saw each other at different Starbucks across the street from each other." This scene epitomizes the proliferation of the Starbucks franchise.

Shultz retired in 2000. Then the recession hit, and Starbucks saw its fortunes dip for the first time. The company closed stores and postponed plans for expansion. But, in addition to the economic downturn, Starbucks lost its way due to a lack of focus on the coffee, the product that started and drove it all.

Howard Schultz came out of retirement in 2008. He closed every Starbucks store for a morning to retrain baristas how to make the perfect espresso. They lost the smelly breakfast sandwiches and went back to their roots: good coffee. The company soon regained its momentum and continued its expansion. Shultz retired for a second time in 2016.

I'm not entirely sold. While Starbucks has retained its emphasis on coffee and the coffee house experience, the company still chases sexy from time to time. It dabbled in areas such as music and alcohol sales. I worry the focus will wander and the coffee will suffer. Plenty of competitors are ready to wear the coffee king crown.

Take Blue Bottle Coffee, for instance. The high-end coffee retailer opened in Oakland, California, in 2000 and has steadily expanded to roughly 50 cafes in large cities in the U.S. and Japan.[51] Blue Bottle sells so-called "third wave" coffee drinks, a notch above Starbucks' "second wave" beverages, thanks to higher quality beans, direct trade with growers, single origin batches (no blends), and fancier coffee making machines. Blue Bottle isn't going after the entire Starbucks crowd (at least not yet). The company is attempting to corral the coffee snobs the same way craft breweries roped in the beer aficionados. So far, so good.

A friend recently told me about a trip to a Blue Bottle Cafe in New York. The coffee was delicious, he said, so good he wished to purchase beans and make it at home. He wanted a pound of beans but could only find them in smaller

[51] "Who We Are: Blue Bottle Coffee." *Coffee Roaster—Brewers, Subscriptions & Brew Guides—Blue Bottle Coffee*, https://bluebottle-coffee.com/our-story.

portions. So he picked up two bags and asked the barista to grind the beans for him, griping a bit as he paid. She politely explained that the beans came in smaller portions to better ensure freshness and that Blue Bottle didn't grind beans on site because they believed their coffee should be ground immediately before brewing.

"Can you believe it?" said my friend.

"Yes, I can," I replied. "From a business standpoint it makes perfect sense. It doesn't want to dilute their brand or lose their target audiences. The minute they start making sacrifices, no matter how trivial they seem to you, they loosen their hold on the top end of the market. They have found their niche and are implementing a focused mission. They are resisting the temptation to chase sexy."

SUMMARY POINTS

- "Chasing sexy" is a common tendency that entrepreneurs and "me" business leaders have. They focus too much on the "next million-dollar idea" instead of concentrating on the parts of the business that have brought them success in the first place. This corporate ADD can lead to confused staff, muddled messages to customers, and big drops in performance and profit.
- To resist chasing sexy, first craft an anti-mission statement (listing everything your company is not) then a clearer, more focused mission statement (losing all the jargon and useless platitudes).
- Put that enhanced mission statement to the test with an Ebenezer Scrooge evaluation. Does it stand the test of time—past, present, and future?
- Finally, put the mission statement into practice and action, making sure the message and focus permeate every function of your company.

Visit Collaboration-LLC.com for a whitepaper strategic plan versus implementation plan and webinar titled, "Core Elements of Strategic Planning."

E-MYTH BUSTING

Whenever I meet with startup business leaders, I ask them their goals. Most are cautiously optimistic. They have big dreams, but they understand the challenges of their markets and all the hard work ahead.

Some feed me a big slice of pie in the sky. They want to be retired multi-millionaires by age 25 or sell their unfinished product to Google for a fortune within the year.

Some want to be on *Shark Tank*. "Noooo!" I want to scream. If you're looking for fantastical entertainment, *Shark Tank* is a wonderful show. But if you're looking for instant riches or management ideas, turn it off. Immediately.

Listen, I love fairytales as much as anyone. And the entrepreneur is our modern-day dragon slayer. But the media portrays entrepreneurs the same way they cover the lottery. They love to showcase the lucky souls who strike it rich. Big checks! Plans to purchase yachts and mansions! What they don't focus on are the millions of others who cast their lot and came up short.

I get it. We all cheer for long shots who make it big. We want to be inspired. But at some point, we start to believe that every long shot has an excellent chance to make it. Hard work and brilliant ideas will always prevail! We gloss over the facts and embrace the fantasy of entrepreneurship. We launch businesses with our brains full of misinformation and naivety. I say "we" because I certainly did.

What happens next? We immediately realize the conventional wisdom surrounding entrepreneurship couldn't be more wrong. The challenges we face are far more daunting, and the workload is exponentially more than we thought. We scramble to adjust and vow to work even harder. It feels like everything needs to be changed—timelines, markets, products, expectations. We look at a magazine cover or turn on CNBC and see a smiling entrepreneur...then immediately feel worse about ourselves. We ask ourselves, If Elon Musk and Richard Branson are triumphant at every turn (they're not, by the way), why can't I be like them?

If you're going to start a business, I tell clients and prospective clients, it's crucial to bust the myths surrounding entrepreneurship. You deserve the truth. The fate of your business depends on it.

So, between chapters, I'd like to do a little entrepreneurial myth busting.

> **E-Myth: Your startup will succeed**
> **if you work hard enough.**
> **E-Reality: Most startups fail.**

There's misinformation on all sides of the business failure debate. Skeptics regurgitate commonly cited statistics like, "Nine out of ten restaurants go under" or "Eight out of ten startups fail after five years." The reality isn't that grim, but it's sobering nonetheless.

According to the U.S. Bureau of Labor Statistics, about half of all businesses fail before five years, and about two-thirds fail within ten years. The exact number is hard to pinpoint. If a business owner retires and simply shutters his company, is that a "failure"? If a company shuts down operations, then opens its doors as a new company with a new name, is that a failure?

We don't know the exact odds, but we do know they're stacked against us. Even the rosiest statistics show that most new businesses fail. We also know that failure rates are higher for some industries (construction, real estate, food service, technology) than others (health care or education, for example).

Perhaps your company is seeking venture capital (VC) funding. There has been a sharp increase in VC funding over the past several years.[52] This hasn't translated into dramatically increased success rates. Far from it.

Harvard Business School released a study concluding three out of every four venture capital-backed firms failed to deliver projected returns. "The last 10 to 20 years you'd think that it has been all about VCs making money, because that's all we hear about," said angel investor Dave McClure, founder of the Silicon Valley accelerator 500 Startups. "But it's really about VCs failing and failing to return capital and being fucking idiots. VCs are stupid. They are absolutely stupid."[53]

Regardless of the funding source, even if you're fortunate and skilled enough to get your new company up and running, you're still likely to struggle. Only 30 percent of new businesses break even; 30 percent operate at a loss.[54]

---

[52] https://pitchbook.com/news/articles/the-state-of-us-venture-capital-activity-in-15-charts

[53] https://www.theatlantic.com/technology/archive/2012/08/its-hard-out-there-venture-capitalist/324377/

[54] https://smallbiztrends.com/2016/11/startup-statistics-small-business.html

CHAPTER 5

DISTRUSTING TRUST

If you're an entrepreneur, you've probably heard the voices in your head: "My staff doesn't love the business as much as I do." "Every one of them would leave if they ever got a better opportunity." "They'll never work as hard as I do because their name isn't on the front door!"

I not only listened to those voices but carried on entire conversations in my mind before I left for my sabbatical. Prior to the trip, the self-centered entrepreneur in me voiced a lack of trust at every turn: "They're going to screw it up." "I'm the only one who can close the new business deal." "They're too young, inexperienced, apathetic...fill in the blank."

Deep in my brain, a counter voice struggled to be heard: "Teach them. Help them. Grow as a team." I don't think that voice ever won an argument. Instead, whenever I saw an employee do anything less than perfect, I'd jump in and try to do the job myself.

It doesn't take a professional psychologist to see the vicious cycle here. My daily lack of trust was creating a mountain of distrust, something I didn't see until I stepped away from my business. I didn't think I was being dishonest. I was just acting like a go-it-alone entrepreneur instead of a mature, collaborative business leader.

This thinking is common for businesses at any stage of their development. We entrepreneurs are used to doing everything ourselves. We're the ones who scraped together the startup capital, closed those first deals, and pitched our products or services to all who would listen. Now we're supposed to give that all away? Well, that's easier said than done.

It's like being a new parent. You were there for your child from day one, feeding him, caressing him, changing his diaper, worrying over every little scrape or rash. Then several years later, you're supposed to hand your child over to a preschool teacher who doesn't know him, who doesn't love and agonize over him the way you do? If you want your child to grow and mature, the answer is a resounding "yes."

I equate trust in an office to a coat of armor that protects the firm's harmony. Little things business leaders do put dents and chinks in that armor. You choose not to tell your staff about a potential new investor. Chink. You rewrite every press release or new business pitch. Chink. You go off-script during meetings. Chink. In short order, that coat of armor is looking like a cheese grater.

Far too many businesspeople can't make the pivot from skeptical entrepreneur to trusting business leader. Some never delegate. Some do so at first, then micromanage their employees to the point where the words ring hollow. Some make more of an effort but just can't help jumping in, often at the wrong time.

Trust me, the best gift you can give your employees is trust. It's motivating for them, liberating for you, and it's free. Fact: your business will never thrive until you trust those around you. If you have any hesitation, it's time to wage war against those doubts and create a healthier, more collaborative, more successful environment. This chapter will show you how.

DISTRUST IN ACTION

To Richard Edelman, president and CEO of Edelman, the world's largest public relations firm, the importance of trust hit home after watching riots in the streets during the 1999 World Trade Organization meetings in Seattle. Edelman saw the "Battle in Seattle" as a sea-changing moment. His epiphany? Businesses and governments could no longer be successful under old rules that emphasized top-down, need-to-know, military-type operations. A new generation demanded more transparency and interaction. They craved trust.

Edelman grabbed his top lieutenant and his research director and told them, "We need to learn more about trust. How much trust does the public place in governments, NGOs, companies, and the media? Who do they trust as their preferred sources of information?"[55] One year later, the giant PR firm produced the first Edelman Trust Barometer, an international survey that detailed levels of trust in a handful of western countries including the United States. The study found a growing distrust of companies and their leaders. It confirmed we were entering a new era of distrust and miscommunication. Edelman decided to make the survey an annual event,

---

[55] Wisner, *Edelman and the Rise of Public Relations*, page 102

releasing the results at the World Economic Forum in Davos, Switzerland.

"People thought I was crazy, but I wanted the findings to become part of the common language of communications," said Edelman. "I felt that we would all be better off if we knew more about trust."

Now surveying trust in more than 25 countries, the Edelman Trust Barometer has measured growing levels of distrust globally. The problem is that all too few companies are heeding the results of the surveys. Countless companies are still operating by the old rules.

You can plant Forever 21® and its CEO Do Won Chang in this category. At first glance, Chang's rise is the stuff of entrepreneurial legend. He and his wife, Jin Sook, arrived in the United States from their native South Korea in 1981 with little more than a burning desire to better their lives. They landed at Los Angeles International Airport on a Saturday, and by early the next week Chang had secured a job washing dishes in a coffee shop.

It wasn't enough to make ends meet, so he took another job pumping gas. While there, he noticed many of the more expensive automobiles belonged to businesspeople who worked in the garment district. Inspired, Chang shifted to a job at a clothing store. "I treated it like it was my own business, and the boss really liked me," he told *Forbes*.[56]

A few years later, Chang and his wife pooled $11,000 and bought a 900-square-foot clothing store near downtown

---

[56] https://www.forbes.com/sites/gracechung/2016/10/05/exclusive-interview-with-one-of-americas-most-successful-immigrants-forever-21s-do-won-chang/#25ad657542ab

L.A., calling the new venture Forever 21. They experienced success from the get-go, purchasing discontinued garments directly from manufacturers then selling the trendy items at a tidy markup. Forever 21 struck a chord with an under-served market—young, fashion-conscious buyers with limited resources. The entrepreneurs expanded immediately and aggressively. The company soon grew to more than 600 Forever 21 stores around the world, making Chang and his wife multibillionaires. It's an All-American success story!

Or was it a soon-to-be horror story? As the company grew, so did the lawsuits challenging Forever 21's unethical business practices. Designers such as Anna Sui, Gwen Stefani, and Diane Von Furstenberg sued the company for selling cheap, nearly identical knockoffs of their dresses and prints. The company has settled more than 50 such cases out of court.[57]

Bigger problems brewed within the company. Factory workers supplying Forever 21 sued to collect overtime pay and unpaid wages and improve sweatshop working conditions. When the company didn't budge, the workers staged protests at Forever 21 stores and in front of Chang's home.[58] They organized a boycott that lasted three years before Forever 21 finally settled.

In 2012, five former Forever 21 employees filed a class action lawsuit. They claimed they were routinely detained during lunch breaks and after their shifts, without over-time pay, so managers could search their bags for stolen

---

[57] https://jezebel.com/5822762/how-forever-21-keeps-getting-away-with-designer-knockoffs

[58] https://www.nytimes.com/2007/09/04/arts/television/04docu.html

merchandise. At the time, this was part of the company's loss prevention policy.

More recently, Forever 21 avoided providing healthcare to employees by limiting hours and making many full-time employees "part-time" employees. The Affordable Care Act requires healthcare coverage for employees who work more than 30 hours a week. Forever 21 skirted the law by limiting many employees to only 29.5 work hours per week.[59]

Is it any surprise that, according to Glassdoor, Do Won Chang has only a 30 percent approval rating? How would you like to have your bag searched every day? What about being denied a paid lunch break? Or having your hours limited so you didn't qualify for health care? How's the level of trust at Forever 21?

Ironic, because Chang himself waxes poetic about his first job in the garment industry. "I treated it like it was my own company, and the boss really liked me." Sounds like a high level of trust to me. So why doesn't Chang cultivate that same amount of trust at his company?

From my outsider's perspective, he operates as though he never made the shift from an old-rules, trust-no-one entrepreneur to a modern-day, collaborative business leader who realizes trust is paramount in today's business environment. There are plenty of ways to keep track of inventory without checking bags and blaming innocent employees first. If healthcare costs are an issue, have a discussion with employees about what the company can afford. Don't play silly

---

[59] https://www.marketwatch.com/story/forever-21-under-fire-for-shifting-fulltime-employees-to-part-time-1376936367

games with them by limiting hours. You're killing trust. You're killing your company.

Not surprisingly, Forever 21 has begun to flag of late. Though Chang and Sook are notoriously private with the company's finances, journalists and analysts report the company has struggled to pay vendors, seen its credit revoked, and suffered from over-expansion.[60],[61] It has begun to close failing stores in Europe, Canada, and the U.S., while shrinking the size of other stores.[62],[63],[64] If Forever 21 was a publicly traded company, I would short the stock. Immediately.

BUILDING TRUST

Lack of trust isn't limited to Forever 21. It's an issue at nearly every company I see. Certain CEOs will always struggle to trust their employees. They ignore warning signs and don't see trust as a problem. Others recognize the need to improve but don't know how to change their mindset. The healthiest companies just need a few tips on how to maintain and further trust. They know that the most productive work environments are trusting environments.

---

[60] https://nypost.com/2016/04/28/forever-21-is-having-problems-paying-the-bills/

[61] https://www.racked.com/2016/6/28/12051552/forever-21-business-slowdown

[62] https://apparelresources.com/business-news/retail/forever-21-closing-non-performing-stores/

[63] https://www.businessinsider.com/forever-21-hm-which-is-better-2018-6

[64] https://www.chainstoreage.com/real-estate/report-forever-1-seeks-smaller-stores-loan/

I counsel them that it's all about relationships. It's about your actions more than your words. Here's how you can build that trust quickly, easily, and with minimal cost:

1. Full Disclosure

Let employees know what you're thinking. Invite them to a meeting they normally wouldn't attend. Have a big calendar up on the wall so they can see where you're spending your time or give them access to your electronic calendar.

Also, open your books. Wait, what? You want me to allow employees to have full access to the company finances? Well, yes. Tell them you trust them not to disclose the information to outsiders and let them have a look. What's the worst thing that could happen? They see you're in a bit of a cash crunch or have some extra resources sitting around? Great! Because you've just engaged those employees on a deeper level than ever before. They never cared about cash flow in the past, but now you have them thinking about ways to smooth out your financial worries. Maybe they have a clever idea where you can spend an extra dollar or two.

Look, your employees are probably going to find out all the financial information anyway. They'll compare notes on salaries, bonuses, new business, and office expenditures. If they don't have all the information, they'll probably draw a wrong conclusion or two. They won't understand your choices, or worse, they'll resent you for them.

Before my sabbatical, I guarded our company finances with an iron grip. Instead of being honest with my employees, I put on a show. Everything was great! The financial picture was rosy! I shielded them from any hint of bad news.

But that's not a relationship. That's PR. Bad PR. Employees know immediately when you're spinning them and when you're being real.

When I returned from Europe, I decided to open up about our finances. Almost instantly, I saw the results: more proactive suggestions as to how we can grow the business, fewer complaints about spending decisions, more engagement, more problem-solving, more initiative from everyone. The financial disclosures demonstrated my trust in them, and they made that trust pay off.

Entrepreneurs tend to hide information from others. They're too busy getting their business off the ground. Plus, the news is usually bleak. The odds are stacked against the business from the start. Who would ever want to support a business that has only a lottery chance of real success? Those early years are such an uphill struggle that entrepreneurs even withhold information from themselves! Letters from the bank sit unopened. Rejection emails go right in the delete column.

That's not a problem. To be a successful entrepreneur, you can't fixate on the massive challenges ahead or the overwhelmingly slim chances of success. You'd just depress yourself. Instead, the best entrepreneurs focus on the moment, one day at a time.

The real problem arises after the business takes flight. Some entrepreneurs spend years withholding, trusting no one, and doing everything themselves. It's tough to break those habits once the business has matured and evolved. Full disclosure forces entrepreneurs to begin to do so.

2. Little Actions, Big Results

To build trust, a business leader can take all kinds of simple steps that cost little to no money but produce huge results.

Start with the layout of your office. Is it closed off or does it have a feeling of openness? Are there communal spaces where folks can work together, or are employees required to work at their desks all day? Is there any way you can reconfigure things to make the space feel more collaborative? Sometimes that's as simple as keeping your door open.

Speaking of which, what's your office policy? Do you snarl at employees when they interrupt you, or do you encourage them to approach you at any time? A good compromise is establishing set times when you're free to discuss any issue they have on their minds.

Next, take a look at the schedule to see where tweaks can be made to please employees, boost output, and build trust. Do you offer flexible hours or work-from-home options? What about flexible vacation time? I used to have a bias against these things, having spent most of my early career in traditional corporations. I wanted to see people at their desks, damn it! It was only later that I learned a little flexibility can result in a healthier work environment and a lot more productivity. That single mom who is allowed to leave a little early each day to pick up her child is going to work harder and happier both during the day and when she's away from the office. She'll get her work done and then some.

Talk to your team about their needs and desires. Maybe someone dreams of taking a month-long trip to Africa but only has a week of vacation stored up. Work together. Give them the extra time, but at a time that doesn't hurt the company. Give them partial pay but make a slight tweak to your insurance policy so that they're covered while abroad. Employees will pay back your generosity and flexibility in spades with increased productivity, loyalty, and trust.

There are countless ways you can work collaboratively so that everyone comes out ahead. If you're struggling with this, hire a consulting firm to conduct a professional collaboration assessment and create a plan of action. The results will pay for themselves right away.

Finally, make sure you stock your office with little touches that build trust. I'm talking about things such as free coffee or snacks. I cringe whenever I walk into an office and see a money jar for coffee. If you're going to nickel-and-dime employees on coffee, they're going to nickel-and-dime you on effort. Pay for coffee. Buy pizza when people are working late on a project, or for no reason at all. Pick up the tab.

Give employees free rein to decorate their space as well Allow them to listen to music, so long as it doesn't disrupt others. Loosen up on bringing kids to work. Their trust—and productivity—will flourish.

3. Care to Do More

The aforementioned methods set the stage for the biggest trust booster of all—building a relationship with your coworkers. A meaningful relationship. One crafted from honesty, empathy, and good faith.

Maybe you balk at the thought of opening your books, you're convinced the office layout is fine, and the thought of employees bringing dogs to work gives you the hives. Well, set that stuff aside for the time being and do one thing: start having meaningful conversations with your staff. Learn about their goals, fears, passions, and other important aspects of their lives. Listen more than talk.

Do you know how many bosses take the time to have regular, thoughtful conversations with employees? Very few. In my experience, less than 10 percent. That's shocking. Especially when you know the cost is nothing and the payoff is huge. If I told you that making a free, simple change would boost productivity by 10 percent, would you do it? Of course you would.

Most business leaders I meet hesitate to reveal information or get personal in the office. They're steeped in old-school methods in which bosses talked and employees followed their directives. They follow the "need-to-know" rule. Those methods are no longer relevant, and the need-to-know rule is dead. Ways of interacting have changed. Access to information has changed. Social media, Glassdoor, salary surveys, financial websites, and many other tools have unveiled businesses more than ever before.

Employees not only like this, they crave it. They demand, and deserve, to be treated like equals and fellow human beings, not like replaceable robot parts. So politely ask them about their family, their interests outside of the office, their dreams. I'm not suggesting you pry them for information. Just take the time to listen to whatever they feel comfortable sharing with you. Allow them to set the parameters. Hear what they have to say.

Sometimes a boss will come off as a progressive, caring individual in a job interview, then change into a traditional, detached leader as soon as the person is hired. Employees then feel they've experienced an emotional bait and switch. They become confused, disappointed, and less trusting.

If during their interview an employee talked about their kids or their charitable activities, keep asking them about their kids as long as they're on staff. Even better, maybe there's a way you can help them (time off to go watch a school play or coach a Little League team) or give their charitable efforts a boost (matching funds or paid time off to volunteer). A little care and attention will go a long way.

This entails a bit of opening up from you as well. It's a tough transition for most entrepreneurs to make. In the early stages of a company's development, entrepreneurs frequently sound like a circus barker: "Step right up to the greatest show on Earth! We're going to change the world!"

Mature business leaders know employees don't want a bunch of puffery. After they've heard it a few times, they stop believing it. They don't want a PR spin, they want to be treated honestly, openly, and as equals. Who would you trust more—a boss who says everything is perfect or one who tells you about the challenges ahead?

- Entrepreneurs focus on building a business. Collaborative leaders focus on developing relationships to build the business.
- Entrepreneurs need to have all the answers. Collaborative leaders admit when they don't know something; they know when and how to ask for help.
- Entrepreneurs are threatened by others. Collaborative leaders trust the team around them.
- Entrepreneurs are consumed with results. Collaborative leaders know a good process will lead to strong results.
- Entrepreneurs are quick to blame others. Collaborative leaders focus on problem-solving.
- Entrepreneurs question motives. Collaborative leaders trust they've hired people who mean well.
- Entrepreneurs take over when a job isn't done properly. Collaborative leaders take the time to teach.
- Entrepreneurs operate by their own rules. Collaborative leaders follow the rules that apply to all.
- Entrepreneurs change the rules on a whim. Collaborative leaders stick with the rules.

- Entrepreneurs break promises. Collaborative leaders know that broken promises lead to shattered trust.

4. Building Trust Through Technology

Unless you've been in a cave (or a biodome) recently, you've probably noticed the new ways coworkers communicate with each other. We've shifted from chit chats to texts, face-to-face meetings to virtual meetings, reality to virtual reality.

Whether you're a traditionalist who refuses to plug in to today's wired world, a tech nerd, or someone in between, it's crucial to understand that employees and colleagues rely on devices and technology to communicate, and increasingly so. If you want to reach them, to strengthen relationships and build trust, you can't view technology as the enemy.

I frequently hear complaints about technology, usually from managers and CEOs who see their employees constantly on their devices and don't trust that they're spending that time doing their jobs. Instead of having a discussion with them, they conclude their staff are wasting countless business hours on Facebook posts, Instagram, Snapchat™, TikTok™, and Candy Crush.

The first step is talking with your staff to find out which devices and platforms they use to communicate and which ones are essential for their jobs. You might think your new public relations manager spends too much time on social media. But maybe she's connecting with journalists or subtly spreading the word about your company products. Talk to her about her goals and tactics to reach them. On the flip side, let your staff know that games, internet shopping, or personal indulgences are only allowed on their own time. Be specific.

After you've gotten a handle on employee habits and desires, determine what you feel is the best policy for your company. Take, say, using computers and smartphones in meetings. I have clients who ban this outright. They wish their staff to be fully engaged and take notes on paper. Conversely, I have clients who place no limits on devices. They believe their employees are more productive with their technology in hand. Then I have clients who carve a middle ground, allowing computers in meetings but only to take notes or look up information if necessary. Craft policies that are fair to all, then be consistent. If employees see you breaking the rules, they'll be much more likely to break them as well.

See the process as a give-and-take, one that builds trust on all sides. Where can you give a little? Perhaps you have always used email as your primary means of communicating. If your younger staff don't always respond as quickly as you wish, try texting, group texting, or instant messaging, especially for little questions or comments that can be answered with a word or two.

In addition to texting and emails, I'm a big fan of having a team platform such as Teams™, Basecamp™, Slack™, or Huddle™ where all employees can track projects, share files, or just get a better idea of what everyone else is doing. Make sure everyone gets into the habit of checking the platform before meetings.

5. Meetings and Expectations

Ah, the dreaded meetings. Most entrepreneurs I know hate meetings. They see them as a waste of time, as meaningless exercises that don't help the bottom line. At the same time, most entrepreneurs I know are awful at meetings. They attend them erratically, prepare little, talk more than listen, veer off topic, dismiss suggestions, and walk away from meetings continuing to do whatever they want, even if it goes against the group consensus. No wonder so many employees have a bias against meetings.

There's a common-sense middle ground: fewer meetings, better meetings.

Entrepreneurs are correct in that far too many meetings wander off topic or fail to result in meaningful action. But they need to understand that they're part of the problem.

To correct this issue, first trim meetings down to only the most essential ones—the weekly sales meeting, for example. See where you can move conversations from a meeting room to an online forum. Product development meetings are a good example of this. Instead of having people brainstorm in a room together, have them comment online.

After you've pared the meeting schedule down to a minimum, reduce meeting times as well. Businesses often round up their meetings to the hour. As a result, meetings that should last 20 minutes often last 60. What's wrong with scheduling a 20-minute meeting? Or try an odd number. If 11 minutes is all you need, schedule an 11-minute meeting. Your staff will be amused at first. They'll then pay much closer attention to the time, not wanting to exceed the time limit.

Once the meeting is scheduled, start it on time. Always. Tell your staff that you're going to cut down the number and length of meetings, but in return, everyone is going to show up on time, ready to tackle the agenda.

The best way to do this is by sending out the agenda ahead of time. This speeds up the meetings by giving everyone a running start. I like the Amazon technique of including in the agenda a list of questions that need to be answered.

Once the meeting begins, don't allow "agenda creep" to set in. If colleagues begin to wander off topic, quickly bring them back in line by suggesting they add it to a future agenda. You'll be surprised how many of these agenda items fade away.

It's important to have one person dedicated as the "meeting general," an employee who makes sure the agenda and time limits are followed, the decisions are summarized, and the next steps are understood by all. If a company has an employee who tends to ramble on during meetings, I sometimes encourage them to make the rambler the "meeting general." It's remarkable how often this technique works.

If there's a pressing issue, tackle it first. Get to the heart of the meeting. That way, in case you do run over time and people need to leave, you'll have addressed the main concern. Leave the little stuff for the very end.

Also, make sure to end the meeting with clear and established action items for attendees. Have the moderator sum up with these items. Write them on a white board or post them online. That way there will be no confusion as to responsibilities and timelines.

Once the agenda and action items are covered, end the meeting. If you feel people aren't ready or prepared enough for the meeting, cancel it—even during the meeting. It's especially important to cancel if it's your meeting and you're the one who isn't prepared! Your coworkers will respect you and trust you more if you don't waste their time.

I'm also a fan of the mini meeting, a quick huddle around someone's desk instead of a big production. I also like it when issues can be covered over the phone rather than waiting for everyone's schedule to align for an in-person meeting.

Studies show that our brains work best between about 9 a.m. and noon. So, schedule meetings that require the most amount of analytical thought and precision in the mornings. We slow down a bit after lunch, but then we pick up energy mid-to-late afternoon. If you can't meet in the morning, 4 p.m. is better than 2 p.m.[65]

---

[65] https://www.npr.org/2018/01/17/578666036/daniel-pinks-when-shows-the-importance-of-timing-throughout-life

Finally, keep it simple. Lose the introductory games and icebreakers. You don't need to have donuts at every meeting. We don't need a report from everybody in the room. Cut to the chase, cover the subject at hand, and build trust in the process.

6. Constantly Take the Pulse

Trust is high maintenance. It requires constant care and attention. Even if business leaders take the steps necessary to build trust within their organization, old habits often return unless those leaders constantly assess the bonds they've established.

Sometimes this is as easy as pulling a colleague aside from time to time to hear feedback about, say, the new technology tools or meeting formats. Hear what they have to say and be open to tweaks. The question you should be asking them ad nauseam is, "How can I help you do your job?"

Besides one-on-one conversations, gather feedback through quick surveys or votes, either in person or electronically. Gather anonymous feedback via a tool such as TINYPulse™ or Office Vibe™, which survey employees on how they're feeling about their jobs. Or hire a professional business consultancy that specializes in strengthening organizational relationships.

TRUST IN ACTION

David DeWolf is the CEO of 3Pillar Global, a software company with 700 employees worldwide. DeWolf likes to wander through the company's offices, talking with rank-and-file employees. He feels he learns much during these informal chat-and-listen sessions.

Several years ago, DeWolf began hearing a growing number of complaints from his workers, ranging from trivial matters to more pressing concerns. The barbs were usually directed from one section of the company to another. He observed that workers in one division didn't know what employees elsewhere in the company were doing. DeWolf concluded that the company had a communication problem on its hands.

But after talking to more colleagues and digging a little deeper, DeWolf realized he was dealing with something much more serious and overarching—a lack of trust. Divisions didn't communicate with each other because they didn't trust each other. DeWolf decided he needed to do something fast before the distrust took deeper root. He fashioned a plan similar to the action items in this chapter.

First, he shared what he had heard and observed. He told his employees he didn't want finger-pointing, he wanted to fix the problem. DeWolf took partial responsibility. "I explained that while I was disappointed in them, it was clear my own lack of insight and leadership allowed the issue to deteriorate to the point that it had," he wrote in *Fortune*.[66]

DeWolf knew that trust is fragile. It can be lost in an instant, and it takes significant time to rebuild. He sensed his employees had dug in their heels and were hesitant to change. He realized he needed to do more than just organize

---

[66] http://fortune.com/2015/07/30/david-dewolf-building-trust/

a series of "clear-the-air" meetings. He chose a unique path: vulnerability.

DeWolf started the trust-rebuilding process by asking a Human Resources executive to pinpoint something she didn't like in his leadership style. After a bit of hesitation, and assurances by DeWolf he wanted the unvarnished truth, she told him she felt he could praise employee accomplishments more often.

"I listened intently, and then slowly repeated what I had heard from her, in my own words. After she acknowledged that I had heard her correctly, I committed to her that I would do my best to be more thoughtful in the future. As I expressed my commitment, you could see the relief in her eyes. She was genuinely pleased to have shared her feedback and receive positive reinforcement. The virtuous cycle of trust had been reestablished."

DeWolf's honesty and willingness to change altered the situation immediately. It allowed his team to begin speaking openly about the problems while devising solutions together. It would take time, but DeWolf felt the company was back on track.

SUMMARY POINTS

- A business will never reach its potential unless there is a strong bond of trust between leaders and staff. But trust isn't something developed overnight. It takes time, a strong commitment, and actions to back up the words.
- Trust is also fragile and high maintenance. Inexperienced executives often do little things that destroy trust without even realizing it.
- To build trust, collaborative leaders disclose more information to employees and include them more often. They take actions such as instituting open-door policies or offering flexible schedules. They also strive to better relate to employees on a personal level.
- Additional ways to build trust include conducting better (and fewer) meetings, enhancing communication through technology, and constantly assessing the level of trust throughout the company.
- Novice business leaders focus on building the business. Collaborative leaders focus on developing relationships to build the business.

Visit Collaboration-LLC.com for a whitepaper titled, "Leadership versus Management: Why a Growing Business Needs Both."

E-MYTH BUSTING

E-Myth: Entrepreneurs are big risk takers.
E-Reality: Entrepreneurs are risk averse.

The language we use to describe entrepreneurial activity is the same terminology we use to describe the World Series of Poker. Entrepreneurs "bet the house" on new ventures. They "risk everything" on a new product. They "double down," "call a bluff," "slow play," and "go all in." It makes for great copy...but it's almost always wrong.

Entrepreneurs aren't experts at taking risks, they're experts at eliminating them. Start with Donald Trump, former president and risk-avoider-in-chief. Forget about his politics. Focus on his business record. In the 1980s, Trump operated like a traditional big city developer. He borrowed money, constructed buildings and casinos, then sold or operated the developments. As long as the real estate market trended up, Trump's model made money.

But when the real estate market turned in the late '80s, Trump found himself in a perilous position, owing billions of dollars to the banks. Like any entrepreneur, he scrambled. He sold assets, sent two casinos into bankruptcy protection, and cut deals to limit his personal liability. He survived.

A decade later, he took a different approach. He reinvented himself as a reality television star thanks to the success of *The Apprentice*. Then he used this newfound global fame to license the Trump name for scores of products—everything from fragrances to furniture to real estate. This greatly reduced his risk. He could make millions of dollars without having to take on any debt.

There's a saying that it's better to have a friend with a boat than to own a boat. Trump took this approach a step further: it's better to have a friend who will pay you to put your name on their boat than to own a boat.

Take a close look the next time you see a story about entrepreneurs "risking it all." Are they really? What's the downside of the deal for them?

Malcolm Gladwell attacked this myth from a different angle in an article he penned for *The New Yorker* called, "The Sure Thing: How Entrepreneurs Really Succeed." He looked at entrepreneurs widely seen as risk takers—people like Ted Turner. Turner's television broadcasting empire didn't begin with a big gamble as most people believed. Turner inherited a highly lucrative billboard business from his father. Then he used his position to purchase a local TV station at a price far below market, financing the entire transaction with a stock swap that allowed him to avoid putting any money down. Doesn't sound like a riverboat gambler to me.

"People like (Marcel) Dassault and (George) Eastman and (Bernard) Arnault and Turner are all successful entrepreneurs, businessmen whose insights and decisions have transformed the economy, but their entrepreneurial spirit couldn't have less in common with that of the daring risk-taker of popular imagination," wrote Gladwell.[67]

So forget "No risk, no reward." A more accurate slogan for these entrepreneurs would be "Risk for you, reward for me."

---

[67] Gladwell, Malcolm. "The Sure Thing." *The New Yorker*, 11 Jan. 2010, https://www.newyorker.com/magazine/2010/01/18/the-sure-thing.

CHAPTER 6

MORE EMPOWERMENT TO YOU

You probably don't recognize the name Dal LaMagna, but you may know his alter ego—Tweezerman®.

LaMagna's story is an entrepreneurial classic. After suffering a string of business failures, including the development of disposable tin pans sized to fit lasagna noodles and an attempt to turn old drive-in movie theaters into drive-in discos,[68] LaMagna struck startup gold when he came across a high-precision tweezer used by jewelers to handle diamonds. Realizing the tweezers could be used for other purposes, LaMagna purchased a batch and started selling them first for splinter plucking and then as tools for plucking eyebrows. He improved the design by adding a slant to the tip and dubbed the new company Tweezerman.

---

[68] https://www.businessinsider.com/how-15-failed-businesses-led-the-founder-of-tweezerman-to-a-multi-million-dollar-empire-2010-12

Tweezerman tweezers soon became "must-have" products for beauticians and home consumers. LaMagna offered new designs and partnered with businesses such as Walgreens™ and Bed Bath & Beyond™. A quarter century later, he sold the company to German knife maker J. A. Henckels for $57 million.

LaMagna announced his retirement, but his entrepreneurial spirit remained restless. A self-proclaimed political progressive, he sought to help sustainable businesses that were making a social impact. He joined the board of IceStone®, a Brooklyn-based company that produced designer countertops out of recycled glass and concrete. After the CEO departed, LaMagna took the reins.

LaMagna loved IceStone's products, though he jokes it's much tougher to ship a 2,000-pound countertop than a one-ounce tweezer. But LaMagna soon discovered that while the countertops are sustainable, the company's financial picture was not. IceStone was hemorrhaging $250,000 a month. He had stepped into financial quicksand.

LaMagna believed in the company and the product. Most of all, he believed in the employees, many of them Nepali immigrants. He pulled everyone together and detailed their dire financial situation. He asked for their help and ideas to get costs down. Meanwhile, he convinced shareholders to sell the employees a 10 percent stake in the company. His message was, "We are all in this together."

The employees jumped in with many effective suggestions. The company stretched operating hours, sublet unused warehouse space, sold outdated equipment, and upgraded technology. LaMagna watched the deficit shrink in half.

But just as the financial picture brightened, Hurricane Sandy hit. LaMagna rushed to the Brooklyn facility to find five feet of standing water, rendering much of the equipment inoperable. Rather than give up or wait for an insurance payment, the employees redoubled their efforts. They rebuilt the equipment themselves and helped get the company back on its feet within six months.

IceStone sales began to take off again, and LaMagna repaid his workers. Literally. He and the board decided to pay employees for 40 hours a week, while only making them work 37.5 hours a week. Today, IceStone countertops can be seen in Whole Foods™, Starbucks, NASA, and the Gates Foundation headquarters in Seattle.

"In my younger days, I was the entrepreneur who had the idea and who drove the business. I hired employees to help me," LaMagna told *Inc.* Magazine[69] "Today, I have employees who respect me. They love their work. They work hard. It's very satisfying. I ran into New York City Mayor Bill DeBlasio before he got elected and talked to him about wealth inequality. I told him the most important thing about wealth inequality is to empower employees."

That quote resonated with me. "The most important thing about wealth inequality is to empower employees." I'm guessing it would make most new entrepreneurs cringe or scrunch their faces in confusion. Why on Earth would we want to give our power away?

---

[69] Pofeldt, Elaine. "Why Dal Lamagna of Tweezer-Man Deferred Retirement to Steer Recovery of Icestone." *Inc.com*, Inc., 5 May 2014, https://www.inc.com/magazine/201405/elain-pofeldt/dal-lamagna-hurricane-sandy-recovery-empowered-employees.html.

That's because new entrepreneurs are all about accumulating power. They tend to give little to nothing away. They hoard responsibilities and resources because they think that's the only way to get a business off the ground. Sometimes, they're correct. Entrepreneurs are doers. But as soon as the company establishes itself, that mindset is lethal. It's essential for every business leader to make the shift from doer to leader.

Understanding this concept requires a slight shift in how entrepreneurs see empowerment. I help business leaders do this by asking them to dream, something they do quite well. I ask them, "Where do you want to be in three years, five, ten? Do you still want to be hustling as hard as you are now, or would you rather shift to a higher level of management, one that requires fewer hours? Do you see your company ending as soon as you retire, or do you see it as a legacy business? Do you ever fantasize about working your way out of a job?"

Those dreaming sessions help entrepreneurs step out of the day-to-day grind and into a big-picture mindset. Still, it's a hard mental shift to make. Our tendency as entrepreneurs is to go back to doing every job, insert ourselves wherever possible, and carry the stress of it all. We just can't let it go. We know that anxiety, chaos, deadlines, and problems are an unhealthy diet, but it's a diet to which we've become accustomed. We often don't mind crises because we get a rush by stepping in and solving the problem ourselves. We want everyone to realize that we are the only people who can do things the way they need to be done.

Stop. Listen to the people closest to you outside the office—a spouse, a relative, or your best friends, for instance. Ask them if they think you're overworked, overstressed, a different person these days. I've yet to meet an entrepreneur's spouse who didn't think their partner could cut back a bit. Tell me you've never been reprimanded for checking emails in bed or taking a business call during family time. I didn't think so.

At some level you get it. For the sake of your health, your family, your dreams, and your company's growth, you need to empower others more. Every successful long-term business leader I know has taken to empowering their staff while developing a "leadership pipeline."[70] They've made the shift to empowerment in both thought and deed.

Often the shift comes as a result of a crisis or major challenge. A partner (business or personal) threatens to leave. You land two huge pieces of business and realize you can't serve both. You see signs that you're the bottleneck to your company's growth, a missed sale, or a lost account because the whole operation is waiting on you.

But crisis isn't an optimal precursor to change. It's far better to take an honest look at your operation and proactively make a few changes to better empower others. This can start with your dreams.

Mine is to live in Barcelona in five years. Steve and I love the lifestyle—the aimless strolls and lazy lunches, vibrant beaches, and historic buildings. To get there, I need to work myself out of a job.

But I don't want my company to fold. I want my team to continue to help leaders grow their businesses. I know I'll be

---

[70] "Building Your Leadership Pipeline." *Leadership Pipeline Institute*, https://leadershippipelineinstitute.com/expertise-building-your-leadership-pipeline.

a part of that next iteration, but I'm not sure precisely what my role will be. I just know I want the business to continue to grow and prosper while I'm overseas. When I left on my sabbatical, I didn't care if my company survived. Now I want it to thrive. I want a legacy business.

Before my first extended trip abroad, I shared little with my staff, especially when it came to personal desires and frustrations. "Entrepreneurs don't share feelings!" I told myself. Acting like an entrepreneur was the worst thing I could've done to my employees. Here I was, managing every decision, butting into everyone's job, yet not being open and honest with them about my feelings and desires for the company's future.

This time it was different. I shared with the entire staff my dream of moving to Barcelona. As soon as I told them, I could feel a new energy. They became invested. They offered to learn new skills or take over various tasks. We hired new staff and shuffled responsibilities. Everyone experienced a new level of empowerment. I have no doubt you'll find me on the Spanish shores in five years, but only if I continue to empower those who can make it happen.

THE EMPOWERMENT CHECKLIST

Regardless of whether you fantasize about foreign destinations, want to create a little more balance in your life, or wish that your business grows today and long into the future, here are the steps you must take to empower your empowerment:

1. Challenge Your Mindset, Then Change Your Mindset.

Empowerment equals freedom. Empowerment equals a new level of success. Look around to your favorite CEOs, your entrepreneurial heroes. I guarantee you they've all done a decent job delegating. Warren Buffet will sometimes only chat a few times a year with the CEOs who run his companies. In five years, do you really want to be in the middle of every crisis or pull all-nighters on sales pitches? Don't you envision a heightened role? Empowerment is the only path.

2. Put Your Desires on the Table.

Let your staff know about your dreams. If you're uncomfortable sharing the big fantasies, start with something small like, "I don't want to do any more breakfast meetings" or "I want to work half-days on Friday so I can travel more on weekends." You'll be amazed how quickly your dreams become communal. Often, your staff will devise ways of achieving your goals quicker than you imagined.

3. Develop Your Leadership Pipeline.

Sharing a goal with staff is great. Now it's time to empower the individuals around you who can get the job done without your heavy involvement. This requires a healthy dose of trust and tutoring. Arrange for them to receive job training through a local organization or online. Bring your associates with you to meetings you would normally attend alone. Share the spotlight at events and speaking engagements.

After hosting the first year alone, I started having one of the senior members of my staff cohost our free monthly webinar. I did it to help groom her to one day host the sessions alone if I'm away. But, frankly, I also did it to spice up the webinars with a different presence and perspective. Her inclusion and empowerment have made the events better than ever before.

Another approach is to carve out time for teaching staff yourself. It's a great way to measure when they're able to take on additional responsibility. I know what you're thinking, "By the time it takes me to teach someone, I could just do it." And you might be correct, but only in the very short term. That sentiment is poison to a company; it's not sustainable. Think of the long game. Your investment in training might not pay off immediately, but you'll see results sooner than you think—results that will last.

Yes, mistakes will happen, especially in the beginning. Try to remember this when they do. Stay calm. Breathe deeply. Be patient. Don't try to fix every problem. Teach the employee to fix the problem.

And instead of explaining how to do everything, teach through questions. Expert law school professors use the Socratic Method, asking students a series of pointed questions to help them strengthen their thinking and better solve problems in the future. When colleagues ask how to do something, respond by asking them questions that will force them to think through the process rather than just handing them the answer.

4. When Possible, Outsource.

I can't tell you how many times I've seen entrepreneurs spend inordinate amounts of time on things like website design or heading to the post office each day to mail something. Outsourcing has never been cheaper, easier, or more widespread than it is today. Start locally. Outsource such tasks as shopping, cleaning, shipping, IT, or anything you and your staff hate to do. Most of the time, you can outsource these jobs for a fraction of the cost of hiring someone full time.

But don't stop there. Look across the country and around the world. Create a network of highly recommended virtual assistants (VAs) to handle such jobs as tax preparation and bookkeeping, travel arrangements, web design and search engine optimization (SEO), social media, writing and public relations, research, payroll, or e-commerce. Ask around and read reviews to pick the best VAs out there. Test them out with a small task before handing over the whole job. I have a personal preference for working with experienced professionals who have recently left a large corporation and opened up their own consultancy.

5. Redesign Your Days.

It's hard for entrepreneurs to do this. They see a meeting taking place, for instance, and they want to crash the confab and share every bit of wisdom they possess. Think twice before you do so. You're not only stymying your staff's development but killing your dream.

Instead, step out of the day-to-day operations and allot time for higher-level management functions. Some software programs and apps can track your activities, block out time on your calendar, and make sure you're allocating your days in accordance with your priorities.

Also, travel and explore ways to improve a product or service. Seek inspiration. Reach out to a client or customer and ask them how your company can do better. Stop spending your days bogged down in the details. Strive for a bigger picture. Then set your schedule in a way that ensures you do so.

6. Set Clear Expectations and Parameters.

After you've made the decision to empower your staff and trained them to take on more responsibility, you must provide them with clear, attainable expectations so that all of you will know whether and where that empowerment is working. The more specific these expectations the better. Give them measurable criteria and hard deadlines.

7. Get the Balance Right.

Many successful managers employ a Freedom Scale, a tool that quantifies the level of freedom and empowerment (and, thus, trust) afforded to each employee. Managers assign each employee a level from one to five. Level one employees have the highest level of freedom and empowerment. They complete tasks proactively on their own, then report back to their bosses. Level twos operate largely on their own with some real-time input from superiors. Level threes require a bit more guidance working with managers before deciding on the best course of action. Level fours require permission and more hand holding from their bosses before handling most tasks. Level fives will remain inactive until their superiors tell them exactly what to do.

Freedom and empowerment are often nebulous concepts in an office or organization. The Freedom Scale allows both managers and employees to see where everybody stands. It's a solid framework for delegation, project management, and promotion.

Talk with your longtime employees about the Freedom Scale. Ask where they feel they rank on the spectrum. If you disagree, discuss why. Be specific. Review their past work and point out where you differ in opinion about their operational freedom. Establish actionable steps that the employee needs to take to climb up the Freedom Scale.

Utilize the Freedom Scale for new hires as well. Let them know their initial level. Tell them exactly how you envision their new role as well as the actions they need to take to advance. "I'm hiring you as a level three salesperson to begin. That means we will work together on sales efforts for the next several months. Once I am confident you can handle most sales calls on your own, I will bump you up to a level two."

The Freedom Scale also gives managers and executives a way to take tasks off their to-do lists and delegate them to others. Write down the items that fill your day. Then assign each task a Freedom Scale level of one to five. If you can delegate items immediately, go for it. If you need an employee to rise up the Freedom Scale before you can hand over a job, let them know.

Employees appreciate the Freedom Scale because it not only allows them to see where they rank but is a good way to keep micromanaging bosses at bay. It also helps prevent a superior from typecasting a worker. Companies frequently lose good employees because they can't see the worker's growth. The Freedom Scale quantifies that maturation.

Overall, if your empowerment efforts are not succeeding to the level you wish, go back through the list and make sure you're not skipping steps. Did you make the shift mentally? Have you shared your dreams? Have you tapped the right people to empower and trained them properly? Are you and your staff on the same page in terms of roles and responsibilities?

EMPOWERMENT IN ACTION

Oscar Munoz is a man who knows quite a bit about empowerment. He's the past president and CEO of United Airlines. Munoz took the helm at United during a tumultuous time in 2015, five years after a problem-fraught merger with Continental Airlines. As his first job, he acknowledged and apologized for the post-merger hiccups, including problems with online booking and airport check-ins. He took out advertisements in major newspapers around the country, apologizing to customers and vowing to do better.[71]

---

[71] https://consumerist.com/2015/10/01/new-united-ceo-apologizes-for-5-years-of-merger-related-problems/

While the ads and apologies were geared toward consumers, Munoz had a second goal in mind: take the blame for his employees and give them a clean slate. The problems were the result of poor management, not poor employees, he said. Munoz made it clear that he would do everything possible to improve the situation by empowering United employees and allowing them the flexibility they needed to enhance customer experience.

Then, disaster struck. Munoz, a triathlete and vegan, suffered a heart attack at age 56. He called 911 and thankfully remembered to unlock the front door to his Chicago apartment before blacking out. Paramedics saved him, but he needed a heart transplant, which he later received.

Most CEOs would've retired. Munoz fought back. He returned to work, made peace with the unions, continued to empower employees, and hired the president of American Airlines as his strong number two in command. He won plaudits internally and out. The airline's performance and stock began to tick up again.

But the relationship between empowerment and performance is a delicate one, a dynamic that requires constant reassessment and care. Munoz continued to preach the virtues of empowerment, going so far as to create an advertising campaign featuring flight attendants and bag handlers as superheroes.[72] After a series of high-profile gaffes—including a passenger being physically dragged off an overbooked flight and a French bulldog dying after a flight attendant insisted

---

[72] https://www.forbes.com/sites/deniselyohn/2018/03/28/how-to-fix-united-airlines-culture-problem/

the dog be placed in the overhead bin—many in the media and public saw United employees as villains.

Workers complained that Munoz said all the right words yet didn't back up the empowerment with the level of training and support required for it to be a success. Munoz aced the first half of our empowerment checklist but came up short on the latter part. He knew he needed to do more, so he ordered a new training program called Core4 that taught employees how to best do their jobs while incorporating the company's four core values: safety, caring, dependability, and efficiency.[73]

As the new training and empowerment efforts took root, Munoz refused his annual bonus and allowed his salary to be cut in half to $9.5 million. He did so to demonstrate "accountability and integrity."[74] That's still a lot of money, but a rare and significant gesture, nonetheless. I'm cheering for Munoz and United. He "gets it." Now he just needs to fashion a plan so that his empowerment efforts pay big dividends inside the company and out.

■ → ■

Any entrepreneur balking at the importance of empowerment should read the biography of George Eastman, the founder of Eastman Kodak. Eastman never married or had children. His sole focus remained his work and philanthropy until the day

---

[73] https://www.forbes.com/sites/deniselyohn/2018/03/28/how-to-fix-united-airlines-culture-problem/

[74] http://fortune.com/2018/04/24/united-airlines-ceo-bonus/

he died. He thrived at each, spreading photography to the mass market while giving millions to schools and hospitals.[75]

He treated his employees well but was a compulsive micromanager. "Eastman found time in the middle of an antitrust investigation to badger underlings about Kodak's rubber bands," wrote The *New York Times*.[76] "He hired detectives to check on the loyalty of his salesmen."

The compulsion to do everything took its toll. In failing health, Eastman ordered a physician to draw a heart on his chest. He pulled out a Luger pistol and fired at the target. "My work is done. Why wait," read the note he left behind.[77]

---

[75] https://www.biography.com/people/george-eastman-9283428

[76] https://www.nytimes.com/2015/03/22/business/at-kodak-clinging-to-a-future-beyond-film.html

[77] "If Your Work Is Done, Why Wait?" *Professor Walter's History Lessons*, https://www.professorwalter.com/2012/01/if-your-work-is-done-why-wait.html.

SUMMARY POINTS

- Entrepreneurs and executives who have grown a business frequently have trouble handing over responsibilities to others. This kills a company's potential growth and overall morale.

- Often, only a crisis or a major event jumpstarts empowerment—a health scare or a large piece of new business, for instance. It's far better to be proactive when it comes to empowerment and implement a plan of action immediately.

- Start by changing your mindset to see empowerment as freedom, as a way for you to achieve your dreams. Make your desires known and build a leadership pipeline of employees who can help make those dreams a reality.

- Outsource when possible and redesign your days to allow you to better focus on the big picture. Set clear and realistic expectations for your staff, and consider using the Freedom Scale, an effective tool for quantifying levels of responsibility within the company.

Visit Collaboration-LLC.com for a whitepaper titled, "Best Practices to Successfully Lead Your Management Team."

E-MYTH BUSTING

> **E-Myth: Entrepreneurs go it alone.**
> **E-Reality: Entrepreneurs rely heavily on others.**

Ted Turner inherited a highly profitable billboard company from his father. Donald Trump received hundreds of millions of dollars from his father to launch his real estate business.[78] They both also relied on their fathers for business connections, support, and helpful advice. They're not outliers. Almost all entrepreneurs get financial support and other forms of help from family members, friends, and business associates.

If you're thinking about starting a business, eliminate the image of going it alone, and start seeing your quest in terms of a collaborative effort.

> **E-Myth: To start a business, you need lots of money.**
> **E-Reality: To start a business, borrow and spend as little as possible.**

Forget about VC funding or large bank loans. Odds are you aren't going to get a dime out of them. You wouldn't want

---

[78] https://www.nytimes.com/interactive/2018/10/02/us/politics/trump-family-wealth.html

that money anyway. It would come with far too many restrictions and deal-with-the-devil conditions.

More than half of the companies on the Inc. 500 list started with less than $5,000.[79] Half! Two-thirds of all businesses start out of a house. That's smart business. They started small, limited their debt, and tested the market to see whether their businesses were viable.

Take your cues not from the Quirkys of the world but from MailChimp®, Maglite, Subway®, and Cards Against Humanity™—companies that started with little money, carved out a niche, produced a good product, then reaped the rewards.

[79] https://www.forbes.com/sites/theyec/2015/01/28/5-myths-about-building-a-million-dollar-business/

CHAPTER 7

CAN'T-MISS COMMUNICATION

To be fair, the odds were against former Yahoo!™ CEO Marissa Mayer from the beginning. But her acting like an entrepreneur made the situation much worse.

Yahoo!'s meteoric rise and disastrous fall is Shakespearean in scope with a mountain of entrepreneurial what-ifs, second-guesses, brilliant innovations, and missed opportunities. Stanford engineering students Jerry Yan and David Filo founded the company in 1994 after experiencing difficulty searching the internet for sports statistics. They created a directory with categories and called it "David and Jerry's Guide to the World Wide Web." The creation was a hit. Make that millions of hits from users starving for a better way to surf the internet.

Yan and Filo wisely changed the company name to Yahoo!, which they joked stood for "Yet Another Hierarchical

Officious Oracle."[80] They continued to make brilliant decisions in the years to follow, taking the company public in 1996 with an $848 million valuation. Within five years, that number would grow to $125 billion, making Yahoo! bigger than Disney™, Viacom™, and News Corp…combined.[81] An iconic series of advertisements ended with the yodeling tagline, "Ya-HOOO-ooo!" Fitting, as the company had scaled to stratospheric heights.

Filo and Yan seemed to be light years ahead of the rest of the digital world. Yahoo! pioneered cloud storage long before Dropbox and offered Yahoo! TV before YouTube, Yahoo! Music before Spotify®, and Yahoo! Notebook® before Evernote®. Pick a category, Yahoo! led the way.

Had Yahoo! focused on just one niche, shifting from an entrepreneur's mindset to a collaborative business mindset, the company might've continued to dominate. Instead, Yahoo! leadership "chased sexy" and failed to capitalize on any of its numerous innovations.

Then came a series of massive setbacks, both external and self-inflicted, beginning with the dot-com crash of 2000. Two years later, Yahoo! had a chance to purchase Google for $5 billion. Yahoo! leadership passed. They also missed out on efforts to purchase eBay, YouTube, and Facebook. Instead, they spent billions acquiring companies such as GeoCities and Broadcast.com—expensive failures. The company took a nosedive.

---

[80] http://money.cnn.com/gallery/technology/2015/03/03/yahoo-20-years-hits-flops/10.html

[81] https://www.fastcompany.com/40544277/the-glory-that-was-yahoo

But companies large and small pull out of downward spirals all the time. Smart business leaders learn from mistakes of the past, reinvent, and start anew. Yahoo! needed to look just across the Silicon Valley to Apple, which had faded into obscurity after Steve Jobs left. He came back with a clearer mission, laser focus, and an honest evaluation of the past. The brand took off again. Same with Best Buy™, Lego™, Old Spice™, Marvel Comics™, and Pabst Blue Ribbon™.

Maybe this is happening at your company. You experienced early success, only to see it crumble. Or you've stalled while competitors have flourished. In addition to redefining your mission, you probably need to recreate your culture.

I've never worked with a struggling company that didn't have a communication problem and, in turn, a culture problem. When companies don't meet expectations, executives often blame employees for botched execution. Workers gripe about poor management decisions or inferior products. Everyone spends their time pointing fingers instead of communicating effectively. If the problem isn't addressed, the damage takes root and becomes irreparable.

This is exactly the situation Marissa Mayer inherited… on a huge stage. She took on a large, iconic company with many high-profile failures at a time when growing competitive giants, including Google, were devouring market share. She also assumed added pressure by being one of the few female CECs in an industry dominated by men. She knew she had to make big changes to turn the company's fortunes around.

Her selection earned raucous applause. Mayer had the skills and background to right the ship. She joined Yahoo! from Google, where she'd been the company's 20th employee, rose to spearhead the core search business (then later Gmail™ and Google Maps™), and earned a reputation as a whip-smart tech leader of the future. She did it with glamour and style, appearing in photo shoots for Vogue and at red-carpet events across the country.

Mayer immediately took steps to restore Yahoo! to its preeminent position. She assembled a new management team and gave the website an overhaul, adding content and shedding money-losing initiatives. She purchased Tumblr™, the micro-blogging and social media site, for $1.1 billion and revamped Flickr™, the company's photo-sharing service. Wall Street applauded. During Mayer's first year as CEO, the company's stock nearly doubled.[82]

But the picture was not nearly as rosy inside the company. A series of ill-considered and poorly explained actions damaged communication and had many employees heading toward the exit doors.

Mayer caused serious dissension when she unilaterally canceled telecommuting, requiring employees to return to an office.[83] Workers complained they had purchased homes and established lifestyles based on being able to telecommute. They claimed they were far more productive working from home. Now they either needed to drive long distances on crowded freeways or quit. Why weren't they consulted before the decision was made? And why the one-size-fits-all approach? Competitor Google allowed workers

---

[82] http://www.businessinsider.com/yahoo-marissa-mayer-rise-and-fall-2017-6

[83] https://www.forbes.com/sites/petercohan/2013/02/26/4-reasons-marissa-mayers-no-at-home-work-policy-is-an-epic-fail/#7ee357b72246

to telecommute on a case-by-case basis, they argued. Why couldn't Yahoo! do the same?

Mayer caused more internal discord when the company began grading workers on a curved, so-called "stack ranking,"[84] then a common practice in Silicon Valley. Yahoo! forced their managers to give a certain percentage of their employees failing grades, even if their performance was satisfactory. Word of the stack rankings quickly began leaking to the press via Yahoo!'s internal message board. Managers complained about having to give arbitrary ratings to employees who deserved better.

Mayer also took heat from employees and the public when she announced she would take only two weeks of maternity leave after the birth of her twins and instead built a nursery in her office and brought her kids to work, a practice banned for all other employees.

Unsurprisingly, workers left the company in large numbers, resulting in a brain drain. Only a third of the remaining workforce had faith in Mayer's leadership, according to Glassdoor. She was named the "least likable" CEO in tech.[85] Employees mockingly called her Evita, a reference to the power-hungry and dictatorial Eva Peron.[86] Ouch.

Did Yahoo! need a major shake-up? Yes. Were all necessary executive actions going to be universally popular? Of course not. Big changes needed to be made. Where Mayer

---

[84] https://hbr.org/2015/01/what-marissa-mayer-got-wrong-and-right-about-stack-ranking-employees

[85] https://www.cnbc.com/2017/05/31/why-yahoo-ceo-marissa-mayer-is-the-least-likable-ceo-in-tech.html

[86] https://www.nytimes.com/2016/01/11/technology/yahoos-brain-drain-shows-a-loss-of-faith-inside-the-company.html_r=0

failed was in her choice to make them alone. She failed to communicate, a common affliction for the entrepreneur.

"From day one, Mayer could have talked less and listened more," concluded *Forbes*.[87] "She could have taken the time to learn before acting (solutions that precede understanding usually don't end well). She could have mended fences rather than building walls. She chose to pontificate, posture, and spin rather than listen, learn, and understand. One of the first things a newly seated chief executive needs to tackle is building trust across all constituencies, but particularly with the workforce. There's an old Roman saying, 'He who controls the army wins'—Mayer lost this battle in the early days."

Take her telecommuting decision as an example. Mayer knew she had a problem with underperforming workers. Making everyone come to an office seemed like an obvious solution. That's how the military would do it. Yet a better, more collaborative approach would've been to present employees with the problem, then solicit their input on a solution. Communicate before, during, and after a policy change. The more inclusive the process, the better the solution. Good communication is important during growth times. It's a matter of life or death during down years.

Problems continued to pile up under Mayer's leadership. Yahoo! struggled to regain its share of the search market. Then it experienced the largest known security breach of a company's computer network. Compounding the problem, the company waited years to admit that all three billion Yahoo! email accounts had been compromised, which

---

[87] https://www.forbes.com/sites/mikemyatt/2015/11/20/marissa-mayer-case-study-in-poor-leadership/?sh=1f730e3a3b46

further damaged Mayer's credibility inside and outside the corporation.[88]

The company became so weak and damaged, it had little choice but to throw up a white flag and sell to a competitor. In 2017, Verizon purchased Yahoo! for $4.48 billion. Mayer resigned as CEO.

She left with a mixed legacy. Yahoo! shares more than tripled during her tenure. But her lack of collaborative communication severely damaged her legacy—and the company's fortunes. We don't know if anyone would've been successful in restoring Yahoo! to its glory days. We do know that any effort to do so would fail without strong internal communication. Mayer needed her employees to fight the battle of turning the company around. Instead, she lost them in droves, largely due to a failure to communicate.

ENHANCING COMMUNICATION

Poor communication is the number one reason people seek to hire my firm. Most business leaders come to our office believing they're doing a decent job with communication but desiring a "few tips" on how to improve. They want their employees to "better understand the company mission" or to "take more initiative without [them] having to explain everything." They often explain it's the employees who need to improve communication. "I have no idea what they are doing," many say.

---

[88] https://www.nytimes.com/2017/10/03/technology/yahoo-hack-3-billion-users.html

Some talk as if they expect their staff to be mind readers or brain clones. They want staff to share their every thought and impulse...but don't want to spend a lot of time on communication themselves.

The employees convey a different view. Poor communication is the top complaint we hear when we conduct employee surveys and focus groups. They confess to having little to no idea what is going on inside their boss's head. They gripe about sudden changes in leadership focus or company expectations. "It feels like we are always playing catch-up," is a common refrain I hear.

Based on my experience, I will almost always side with the employees. It's like a marriage. If one party says there's a problem, there's a problem. Luckily, the situation can be fixed with a few easy yet meaningful steps.

The first thing all sides need to understand is that poor communication is a symptom more than a cause of the company's shortcomings. Let me give you an example.

Say a young entrepreneur has a good idea for a technology product. He spends a year or so bringing that product to market, living and breathing every single detail. The product consumes his waking hours. Like most products, this one probably shifted over time. Maybe a competitor introduced a superior product, or the entrepreneur decided to target a different market. The entrepreneur doesn't have to explain to anyone why he changed course. He just does it.

The product hits the market and experiences some success. The entrepreneur rejoices. He takes steps to rapidly expand the business, hiring a bunch of people to help him achieve his goal. All good.

Except these new staff don't understand the entire evolution of the product. They see a snapshot, not a long and intricate process. They ask questions, but the company is moving so fast, the entrepreneur doesn't have a lot of time to answer all the queries. He grows frustrated that they can't just "figure it out." He hired them to be salespeople or tech support and wants them to "just do their jobs."

A negative culture takes hold. Communication drops to the bottom of the company priority list. Employees do their best to go it alone, though they frequently misstep or misinterpret the founder's intentions. They feel like they're operating in the dark. It's like a married couple who doesn't talk about certain subjects. There are going to be problems. Big ones. It's only a matter of time before things explode.

That's because we tend to get worse in our ways, not better. Without improved communication and structural changes, poor delegators become worse delegators, impulsive leaders become even more shoot-from-the-hip, and absent-minded bosses become even more scatterbrained.

Most business leaders become defensive when we show them the results of our employee surveys and research. They point to open-door policies or inclusive meetings as proof they're communicating well. "That level of communication was fine when you were an entrepreneur," I tell them. "Now, for your business to mature and succeed, you need a whole new approach."

This requires structural changes as well as a shift in attitude. And it will require thorough follow-up and feedback to ensure your communications are on track. Some leaders cringe at the idea of spending more time and resources on communication. They see it as "touchy-feely" or not enhancing the company's bottom line. We have a word for leaders who don't think communication is essential to their company's success: broke.

Need more convincing? Look at the annual Gallup poll on employee engagement, which measures the number of workers who are involved in, enthusiastic about, and committed to their jobs. While engagement levels have crept up a bit of late, only a third of the job force is considered to be "engaged" in their work.[89] It's damn hard to run a company if two-thirds of your workers are apathetic.

Whatever level of communication you think your company needs, double it. Think bigger, broader, more long-lasting. And know that employees put far more credence in your actions than your words. There are three steps you can take to enhance communication: behavioral change, structural change, and follow-up.

Behavioral Change

You're a good person. You mean well. You started your business with noble intentions. Sure, you can always improve communication, but you see your relationship with your staff as decent. And maybe you're right. Maybe you just need to tweak a thing or two. Or maybe you're way off base. You're thinking of a communication tune-up, while your employees are thinking of a major overhaul.

---

[89] https://news.gallup.com/poll/241649/employee-engagement-rise.aspx

You'll never know what, where, and how much you need to improve until you conduct a communications audit. Some business leaders try to do this by reaching out to staff and asking, "How am I doing?" The results are usually mediocre at best. Even if the business leader makes the process anonymous, staff are reluctant to speak openly and honestly for fear of repercussions.

I know I'm plugging my own industry here, but businesses are much better off hiring an outside firm to conduct the audit. A good firm will spend some time looking at all the ways a company communicates, analyzing past successes and shortcomings. They'll do this before reaching out to your staff through either confidential, in-person meetings or electronic communications. The pre-interview research will allow the firm to pinpoint strengths and weaknesses.

It's like the difference between hiring a professional editor and editing your work yourself. We know the professional editor is better, but our egos make us reluctant to hire one. Hire one, a good one.

Try to avoid seeing a professional consulting firm as a bunch of critics. See it as a team of people who are working to make you a better, smarter, more capable leader. See it as a group of professionals who can help make your career and personal dreams a reality.

Still, some leaders cringe at the thought of an audit. They fear a massive gripe session, all directed at them, or they don't see the value added to the bottom line. A professional consulting firm will be able to separate the legitimate complaints from the baseless ones, often changing common perceptions in the process.

The result should be a specific, actionable plan to implement lasting and meaningful change. Experienced consulting firms will offer tried-and-true methods of doing so and positive examples of companies that have faced and overcome similar situations.

Common Communication Complaints and How to Address Them

The following are some of the common complaints we uncover regarding communication, followed by the behavioral changes we suggest:

- **"My boss doesn't listen to me."**

Sometimes this issue can be mitigated with a few simple interpersonal techniques, like ones a relationship counselor would suggest: What is your body language saying when you communicate with your staff? Are your arms folded? Do you look at your phone or computer when conversing with them? Also, how often do you repeat their question back to them to demonstrate you're taking in what they're saying? If they raise a point that you feel is off base, are you dismissive or do you provide constructive feedback?

Make it a point to go into "listening mode" when employees seek you out. Stop what you're doing, set down the phone or fold up the computer, and look them in the eye. These small steps will let employees know that you're receptive to their thoughts. During the conversation, let them take the lead. Ask questions instead of voicing opinions. Try to summarize what they're saying so that both of you are on the same page. Even if you disagree with them, make sure to let them know you hear, value, and need their input. These simple little actions will help build long-term relationships.

• **"I feel like my boss isn't being 100% honest with me."**
Be open and authentic, which includes showing vulnerability or exposing your shortcomings when warranted. Instead of feeding your employees an endless stream of positivity, be real with them. Your team can handle bad news. Tell them you're concerned about an upcoming meeting or product launch. Pay close attention to the written and oral language you use. Do you sound more like a press release or a heartfelt letter? Entrepreneurs focus on popularity; collaborative leaders focus on authenticity.

• **"I feel like there's a disconnect with my boss."**
In his book *Trust Factor: The Science of Creating High Performance Companies*, neuroscientist and author Paul J. Zak breaks down the role certain brain chemicals play in strengthening connections and trust between individuals at a company.[90] When a boss demonstrates trust and understanding to an employee, the worker's brain releases higher levels of the neurotransmitter oxytocin, the so-called "love hormone." The worker becomes, at least for the moment, more empathetic and likely to act. This in

---

[90] https://hbr.org/2017/01/the-neuroscience-of-trust

turn boosts the boss's oxytocin levels, creating a cycle of connection and trust.

What kinds of trust-building activities is Zak talking about? They can be simple things like saying "thank you" when an employee does a favor or "job well done" after an employee does a good job. Zak praises companies that have meaningful awards programs focusing on an individual's growth and performance beyond simple numbers.

You can also demonstrate trust by allowing employees to have a greater say in crafting their jobs and giving them greater discretion in how they do their work. Above all, it's acting a little less like a drill sergeant, and more like a human.

• **"There's a generational gap between my boss and me."**
Unfortunately, businesses do not have access to a "Fountain of Youth." Barring that, it's important for older supervisors to better understand how their younger employees communicate. Younger staff tend to prefer quicker, shorter communiques through texts or social media. They like visual communication—photos, memes, emojis, or movie clips to express a feeling. They also have less of a problem blending their work life and personal life.

Maybe you're more old school. You don't always carry your phone, or you see social media as good for little more than sharing selfies and photos of cats. I'm not suggesting that you become a texting, tweeting, posting machine. I'm saying that if you dismiss all these forms of communication, you're hampering your efforts to bridge the generation gap with your staff.

So find a middle ground. Try texting them instead of emailing from time to time. Social media is a bit trickier. I caution business leaders against following employees on Twitter, Facebook, or Instagram. It can feel invasive, and many companies have policies prohibiting it.

But there's nothing wrong with you starting a Twitter account or Facebook page yourself. Post things such as articles or books you encourage others to read, or photos of company activities. Just make sure the information you post jives with the company mission and avoid mixed messages.

Fact: Many younger employees are much more likely to browse your material through social media accounts on their phone than by reading information you left in their inbox.

On a more personal level, make sure you're not just avoiding new communication methods and that you're not being generally judgmental.

Unfortunately, I see this from time to time. Today's workers have tattoos, hair colors, and body piercings. If you think that makes them lesser workers, think again. By not hiring them, you could be missing out on the best employee you ever had.

• **"I don't always know what I'm supposed to do."**
When communication frays, employees tend to freeze. They don't want to do anything to upset their bosses,

so they end up taking less initiative. They play it safe. This, of course, upsets their bosses. Communication worsens, and the cycle continues spiraling downward.

In our company analyses, we find a frequent culprit: business leaders who focus too much on "what" and not enough on "why."

Say you hire a new sales executive. She has a proven track record with a competitor. *"This will be easy,"* you think when you hire her. *"She just needs to do the same thing for my company as she did with her previous employer: sell, sell, sell."*

Only it doesn't always work out that way. She won't be able to be an effective salesperson until she fully understands why your company is in business. What's the story behind the product? If you don't take the time to share all the details and history of the "why," you're denying her a valuable strategic advantage.

The same goes for all employees. The more you communicate the "why" with them, the more likely they are to take initiative, be effective, and further your company goals. Workers need context as well as clear expectations.

• **"My boss doesn't appreciate me."**
This is the easiest problem to rectify. Carve out a little time each day to say, "Thank you" and "Outstanding job." Make it a point to send a congratulatory text or an old-fashioned note every day. Be specific in your praise such as, "Thanks for organizing the most productive and inspiring corporate retreat we have

ever had." Who among us doesn't appreciate a little praise from time to time? And who among us doesn't start to grumble when we receive nothing but orders and criticisms?

A final bit of behavior advice I give to leaders is to find a communication role model or two. Sometimes this is an old boss. What made them an effective communicator and motivator? Borrow from every one of their techniques. You can also look back at your worst bosses and compile a "How not to" list of items. Swear to never repeat their sins.

In addition, look to outside leaders whose communication skills you admire such as a CEO you heard speak at a conference or a politician who rallied a large crowd. What is it about them that drew you in? If you're still searching for a role model, I recommend *First Break All the Rules* by the researchers at Gallup, a seminal text that examines management techniques across a wide spectrum of leaders.[91] What they have in common is a willingness to toss out conventional wisdom and do whatever it takes to motivate staff and optimize performance.

Structural Change

When you see a sign in a liquor store that reads, "Coldest Beer in Town," do you believe it? Has a bumper sticker ever convinced you to change your opinion about something

---

[91] Buckingham and Coffman, *First, Break All the Rules: What the World's Greatest Managers Do Differently*, 2016.

important? When politicians vow to cut taxes or end poverty, do you put any stock in their words? If you answered yes to any of the questions above, please contact me immediately with your credit card number. I have a can't-miss, once-in-a-lifetime investment opportunity for you!

Our lives are so filled with gibberish and gobbledygook—aka, bullshit—we become anesthetized to the words. We tend to discount huge chunks of what we hear. So when a boss says, "You're always free to make suggestions" or "My door is always open," we remain skeptical. We think, "She says her door is always open, but she never seems to have any free time to talk about my desire for a promotion."

If you're a business leader who's made a few behavior changes to improve communication in your office, great. But you're only part of the way there. You also need to implement structural changes to assure your staff you're committed to building healthy and productive professional relationships.

Take the open-door policy. It's fine to say your door is always open. It's better to set regular hours during which you clear your schedule and do nothing but focus on employees' issues. Or allow staff to schedule a short meeting to discuss anything on their minds, no matter how trivial it seems to you. The matter doesn't matter; it's the meeting itself that matters. And listening is never trivial.

So you tell your staff they're free to voice opinions or make suggestions. Great. Take the next step and include them in more meetings or brainstorming sessions. Instead of waiting for them to speak up, ask them what they think. I know many companies have suggestion boxes (either on-site or online), but my experience is those boxes rarely lead to any substantive change. You end up with a lot of half-baked ideas that are quickly discounted, which results in frustration on all sides.

Ditch the box in favor of face-to-face suggestion sessions. We have a client with more than 130 employees. Management regularly takes five employees at a time out to breakfast for an informal chat session where they can ask questions, make suggestions, or raise any issue they wish. Even if the breakfast sessions don't result in significant change, they're all extremely valuable for strengthening the bonds of communication. Remember, it's not about the end result. It's about a healthy process.

Another way to proactively demonstrate your commitment to strong communication is to go to your employees. Walk around. Meet in their office. Ask if they wish to chat about anything or if they need any help. Sit and listen instead of pontificating.

I'm also a big fan of corporate retreats. If done properly, they create a sense of team and mission, allow folks to ease up a bit, and infuse a little fun in the process. Retreats don't have to be budget busters. Maybe a friend or client has an event space you could use for a day. Go somewhere noncorporate—a winery, campground, art gallery, or large private home.

Technology is also an increasingly important way to enhance corporate communication. My overall advice here is to talk with employees before you go out and purchase expensive equipment or computer programs. Ask them what their preferences and experiences are. Have them test out a program or two. If you involve employees in the decision-making, they're much more likely to use the technology in the future.

Most of the time, less is more when it comes to technology. Instead of buying a bunch of programs, find the one (or two) that best suit(s) your company's needs and focus. For instance, Basecamp is best for project management, while Slack™ is more of a communication and messaging tool. I've seen too many companies go overboard on communication tools, only to leave employees confused and overwhelmed.

I also encourage business leaders to take a look at modern techniques that both large and small companies use.

Google hosts weekly "all-hands" meetings and direct exchanges (via email or in the Google cafes) with senior management. The company makes communication a priority not only as a matter of policy, but also from an architectural standpoint. "Our offices and cafes are designed to encourage interactions between Googlers within and across teams, and to spark conversation about work as well as play," reads Google's About Us page on its website. It also produces a quarterly board report that is distributed to all employees.[92]

Unfortunately, Google experienced an incident that exposed the dangers of some internal communication efforts. CEO Sundar Pichai was forced to cancel an all-hands meeting that was called to discuss a controversial memo penned by a former employee. The employee argued that the gender gap in technology is caused in part by biological and sociological differences between men and women. The memo was quickly panned, both internally and outside the company, as sexist and unscientific.

---

[92] www.wired.com/story/what-googles-open-communication-culture-is-really-like/

Pichai canceled the meeting after the names of several employees who were critical of the memo were leaked to outside organizations, making the employees susceptible to online harassment.[93] He didn't scrap the program altogether, however. Instead, he vowed to improve security and confidentiality so that employees could continue to voice their opinions in various ways at the company. The company has yet to experience a similar breach. "In recognition of Googlers' concerns, we need to step back and create a better set of conditions for us to have the discussion," said Pichai.[94] "So in the coming days we will find several forums to gather and engage with Googlers, where people can feel comfortable to speak freely."

Best Buy also holds quarterly town hall meetings where employees can ask hard questions and voice opinions in person or via the internet. The meetings are structured as a no-holds-barred method of addressing both good and bad news, similar to a political town hall meeting. After a scathing article in *Forbes* that predicted Best Buy would go out of business in a few years, CEO Brian Dunn used the format to set the record straight.

"When I read those things, I feel sort of how you (employees) feel," he said. "I look at it, I get angry. Then I get past my anger and look at these things—what's troubling about it

---

[93] http://money.cnn.com/2017/08/10/technology/business/google-meeting-questions/index.html

[94] https://www.bizjournals.com/bizwomen/news/latest-news/2017/08/google-staff-meeting-canceled-memo-debate-rages-on.html?page=all

is that there are elements of truth to what we're reading and what people are saying and this cries for us to change."[95]

Smaller businesses we counsel use a wide range of tools and resources to enhance internal communication. These include Dropbox, Google Hangouts, webinars, online courses and professional development, newsletters, charity support, multiauthor blogs and crowd-sourced content, and innovative technologies that seem to pop up every day.

I'm a supporter of anything that works for your company. Try them all out. Test them in various situations. Keep the best, discard the rest. Just remember that when it comes to communication, technology can be a real boost, but nothing beats face-to-face contact.

Also, whether in person or online, the platforms should be implemented to maximize communication from all sides, not just to facilitate management speaking to staff. The best collaborative leaders set the long speeches aside to listen, question, and learn.

Follow-up, Feedback, Fine-Tuning

If you're like me, you're getting exasperated with the explosion of customer surveys being requested after every single call or computer interaction you have with a utility, bank, airline, etc. I usually hang up or hit delete.

But as a businessman, I understand the value of surveys. Even if only 10 percent of the callers respond, that's still a lot of useful information. Business leaders aren't as much interested in your individual experience (notice how good some

[95] http://www.inlineproductions.com/best-buy-town-hall-meetings/

representatives are at expressing sympathy...then doing nothing to solve the issue), as they are in big-picture trends: Are we getting better at service or worse? What are the top gripes and how can we address them? How do we stack up against the competition?

Customer surveys can be a turnoff to respondents. Employee surveys are different. Employees are dying to tell you what they think about every inch of your company. Even if you don't listen to a word they say (though you should listen to every word they say), there are enormous benefits to inviting them to participate in a survey. It makes them feel you're serious. It makes them feel they're valued. It lets them get long-lingering sentiments off their chests. It also helps your company master the third essential part of internal communication: follow-up, feedback, and fine-tuning.

You may have vowed to make communication a priority and spent a considerable amount of time and money making sure that emphasis is embedded in your corporate culture. But you can't stop there. Communication is a dynamic garden that requires constant care.

Maybe you slipped back to your old, uncommunicative, typical entrepreneurial ways. Maybe that new computer software program has become a bit outdated. Follow-up and feedback allow you to determine whether you're still on the right path.

An example of this is how we use assessments in our practice. We give our Collaborative Leader Assessment to companies before they implement changes, after those changes have had time to take hold, and annually thereafter. We ask employees and leadership a host of detailed questions about vision, expectations, communication, accountability, development, innovation, balance, and trust. We see how management and worker responses align with each other, how they track over time, and how they stack up against similar companies. We measure trends and pinpoint areas of opportunity.

Then we supplement the quantitative answers with focus groups and one-on-one meetings to better understand qualitative reactions and depth of feelings. This allows us to better identify "make or break" issues as well as ones that are less intense.

At the end of each effort, we share the answers and analyses, and provide the company with a detailed list of action items they can implement on their own, both immediately and over time. We follow up on the results and the company's corrective actions to make sure they're properly addressing the challenges highlighted in the assessment.

The most productive companies are the ones that bring us in year after year. They're the ones that quickly identify any potential problems that are brewing and pinpoint them before they explode. It's like seeing a doctor each year for a check-up. You hope she doesn't catch anything, but if she does, you're glad she caught it early.

SUMMARY POINTS

- Poor communication is the number one reason companies seek help. And I've yet to meet a company that didn't need improvement in this area, especially if the business is stalled or struggling. Whatever level of communication you think your company needs, double it. Think bigger, broader, more long-lasting.
- The three keys to enhancing communication are behavioral change, structural change, and consistent follow-up.
- Necessary behavioral changes include everything from body language and better listening techniques, to sharing more of your reasoning, focusing on authenticity over popularity, embracing the technology preferences of younger staff, and always taking the time to say, "Thank you" or "Job well done."
- Structural changes include open-door policies, informal lunches, face-to-face suggestion sessions, corporate retreats, and "all-hands" gatherings. Also, consider the right technology tools, ones your staff will use and appreciate. Optimal communication requires constant care, so after enacting communication plans, it's time for follow-up, feedback, and fine-tuning.
- Professional assessments and audits can help ensure your communication efforts are on the right track.

Visit Collaboration-LLC.com for a whitepaper and webinar titled, "The Management Dilemma."

E-MYTH BUSTING

> **E-Myth: To start a business, you need
> a revolutionary product or service.
> E-Reality: To start a business, you need
> an evolutionary product or service.**

Any entrepreneur who worries about the lack of a "game-changing" product would be well served to pick up a copy of Mark Twain's autobiography. "There is no such thing as a new idea," wrote Twain. "It is impossible. We simply take a lot of old ideas and put them into a sort of mental kaleidoscope. We give them a turn and they make new and curious combinations."[96]

The same can be said for 99 percent of all the new businesses out there. Electric cars roamed our streets a century ago. Organic, farm-to-table meals have been a staple throughout the history of humankind. Last year's blockbuster toy, the fidget spinner, is a handheld variation of the ages-old top. Strip away the terminology, packaging, and advertising, and you'll probably find a simple twist on an idea someone had long before.

Most startups are in established fields such as food, retail, clothing, construction, and homebuilding. If you teleported

---

[96] https://www.inc.com/stephen-shapiro/stop-worrying-about-novelty-of-your-ideas.

visitors from 50 or 100 years ago to today, they would recognize these new businesses. If you plopped them down in, say, Brooklyn, they might even think they were in a time warp with all the "artisanal pickles," "handcrafted boots," and "small batch whiskey." Zap them 100 years into the future, and they'll probably see another incarnation of the same.

Smart companies know better than to seek revolutionary products. They go after evolutionary products—the ones they can sell as an improvement, however slight, on the current model. Two blades? How about three! Four! This will go on until we feel we've reached a saturation point. Then someone will go back to a model closer to the original idea and we'll start the process all over again. See: Dollar Shave Club®.

The focus on enhancement over "disruption" takes precedence in all sectors, including ones seemingly dependent on revolutionary ideas. Look closely at the tech market. How many of those companies are offering something never seen before? Few, very few. Most of the businesses you'll examine simply make an improvement on a tried-and-true product with proven demand—a faster printer, a simpler messaging app, a more powerful cell phone camera.

You'll also see many companies that have taken an established industry (taxi rides or vacation booking, for instance), realized an opportunity for better market efficiency, and created a new delivery system for the old product (Uber™ or Expedia™). Most e-commerce companies aren't trying to sell you a different mousetrap, they're just trying to get it to you more quickly and easily.

CHAPTER 8

THE HEART
OF YOUR STORY

I'll just come out and say it. With few—very few—exceptions, entrepreneurs are awful storytellers.

They're stunned when I tell them this. "But what about my Ted Talk or my PowerPoint presentation where I promise to disrupt my industry while helping save the world? My new VeggiePresto gizmo will forever change the way people clean and dry lettuce! And with every purchase we will donate a dollar to the Lettuce for Everyone campaign because every person on this planet deserves clean and dry lettuce!"

Um, no, I tell them. Let's work on that a bit.

The last chapter detailed how to best communicate within your company. This chapter will focus on the stories companies share externally.

Let's start with the words and phrases we use. In the world of entrepreneurs, business leaders are "rockstars," a solution is a "hack," self-funding is "bootstrapping," and time is "bandwidth." If this feels like another language, it's because it is. Entreprenuereze, I call it. It may be decipherable to a select few, but to the rest of us it's mumbo jumbo.

The problem is that some entrepreneurs experience a little success with it early on. They use it to persuade an investor to give them a few dollars or to land a sale or two. Then they believe their language and storytelling are fine, so they double down on both.

I've worked with and observed hundreds of startups. Not one of them succeeded because of their jargon and superlatives. I would argue that they succeeded despite them. Just don't try to tell them that.

No, most entrepreneurs who get their business off the ground feel pretty damn good about themselves. They've tasted success one way, and they're going to continue down that path. This is another fundamental sin of entrepreneurship—failure to pivot.

If you want your company to evolve into a mature, thriving operation, it's time to edit your story and alter your approach. It's time to lose the jargon, embrace proven literary storytelling techniques, and get real. Failure to do so will lead to bigger failures ahead.

Here's a situation I encounter regularly. An entrepreneur has a clever new project. He wins a competition and gets a few glowing articles and favorable internet mentions. A handful of investors give him money to hire some people and open an office. He gives his new employees the same song and dance, and they sign up to help.

Then they immediately realize they've been oversold. The product isn't all it's cracked up to be. Competition is much stiffer than they suspected. The new company isn't going to "disrupt" anything.

Worse, the new boss tends to keep pitching the same false tale—always with him hogging the spotlight. The employees are surprised each time they read an article or blog post about him. He keeps promising things they know the company will never be able to fulfill. Time to look for another job.

This entrepreneur has committed numerous costly communication blunders. He made the story about "me" instead of shifting it to "we," the team. Instead of a classic storytelling, challenge-resolution approach, he jumped right to the conclusion. If you picked up a book and read that the hero was perfect, what would you do? I'd put down the book. There'd be no need to become invested because he's got it all figured out on his own.

Collaborative business leaders would pivot and take a different approach. Even before they started hiring, they'd shift the story focus from individual efforts to the greater mission. Anselm Doering did just that.

EMBRACE THE ROLE OF UNDERDOG

A lifelong green business entrepreneur, Anselm Doering found himself out of work after he and his brother had to close their Earth General stores, a two-store chain that sold environmentally friendly house and beauty products in Brooklyn and Manhattan. He stressed about money, especially with his first child on the way. He had no idea how he'd reinvent his career.

Then Doering entered a rest stop restroom on the New York Thruway and saw a poster that changed his life. "Proud to be cleaned with Lysol®," read the advertisement.

"Lysol," he thought. "Lysol is toxic. It's so poisonous it used to be used as birth control. Who would be proud to clean with poison?"

That's when it hit him. Consumers had healthier options when it came to cleaning products with brands such as Method®, Seventh Generation®, and Mrs. Meyer's®. Institutional users didn't have these alternatives. They were stuck with traditional, toxic cleaners and sanitizers. Doering vowed then to create a line of earth-friendly products for commercial users.

Doering got to work, tapping into the product knowledge and connections he had made during his years running the Earth General stores. His father, a biochemist, helped with the formulations that were all plant-based and all effective yet safe on humans, animals, and the planet. He received funding from family and a few green business capitalists. He called the new company EcoLogic Solutions.

Doering could've made his story about him, his epiphany, his new quest. He could've called the new company Doering Detergents. Instead he made it into a team mission. The company's "why"? Help eliminate toxic cleaners in the workplace. The company's "how"? Provide commercial users (restaurants, hotels, offices, and, of course, rest stop restrooms) with a full line of sustainable products. To Doering, sustainability meant competitive pricing and effectiveness as well as positive impact on the environment.

By shifting his story, Doering helped create a cause. People who joined the company immediately saw the mission and felt good about it. Customers identified with the greater good, especially when they learned the earth-friendly products usually cost less and worked as well if not better than traditional cleaners and sanitizers.

Doering talks about "disrupting" the multi-billion-dollar industry but doesn't shy away from the odds EcoLogic Solutions faces. "We're the green David fighting toxic Goliaths," he said. "But every small victory has big returns for our customers, their clients, and the environment.

"I feel like we're helping companies make the shift to sustainability the same way Method and Seventh Generation helped bring green products into the home. The change is happening. More and more companies are embracing sustainability. It's exciting to be a part of that."

Doering embraces the underdog role. He's wise to do so. In storytelling terms, who doesn't root for the underdog? I encourage all other beginning businesses to do the same. If you're up against bigger competition, borrow from the classic storytellers and describe your company using terms they attach to their underdog heroes: hard-working, resilient, resourceful, scrappy, hungry. What you perceive as weakness could easily be turned into a strength.

Dollar Shave Club also welcomed the underdog role. CEO Michael Dubin and his leadership team wanted to cut into Gillette's™ dominance in the marketplace. They determined the whole process of buying razors was expensive and time consuming. Gillette had cornered the market on fancy razors with multiple blades, shields, and other bells and whistles. Dubin and company went the other way. They offered simpler, single blade options, delivered by mail for just a few dollars a month.

Dubin and his team felt they found a niche but struggled to get their message out. They didn't have millions of dollars to spend on advertising like Gillette did. So Dubin made a video in which he walks around a Dollar Shave Club warehouse and makes a humorous pitch for the product, saying things like, "Do you think your razor needs a vibrating handle, a flashlight, a backscratcher, and 10 blades? Your handsome ass grandfather had one blade...and polio."[97] "Do you like spending $20 a month on razors? $19 goes to Roger Federer (Gillette's celebrity spokesperson). I'm good at tennis," he says while swinging a tennis racket and missing the ball.

Dubin estimates the company spent about $4,500 on the video.[98] It went viral, striking a chord with more than 25 million viewers on YouTube. Dubin surmised the reason the video soared was because "...it had a real purpose and a real story. And the reason it hit emotional pay-dirt for people was because there was an enormous amount of frustration. And finally here's something that somebody's doing about this really big problem."

In 2016, British conglomerate Unilever purchased Dollar Shave Club for $1 billion.[99]

ACCEPT THE ROLE OF FAILURE

The wisest, most effective brand storytellers borrow heavily from novelists and screenwriters, embracing humor along with characteristics such as honesty, transparency, and effort. Pixar's number one storytelling rule is, "You admire a

---

[97] https://www.youtube.com/watch?v=ZUG9qYTJMsI&t=1s
[98] http://fortune.com/2015/03/10/dollar-shave-club-founding/
[99] http://fortune.com/2016/07/19/unilever-buys-dollar-shave-club-for-1-billion/

character more for trying than for their successes."[100] That's a great "note to self" for business leaders.

That's also why Nike's® storytelling is so brilliant. University of Oregon track athlete Phil Knight and his coach Bill Bowerman founded the company in 1964. Determined to find an edge for his athletes, Bowerman created track shoes with rubber soles he shaped with his waffle iron. The company has been considered as the athlete's preferred choice ever since. Everything they do is shaped by this mission. They aren't a shoe company; they're an athlete support company. They don't copy; they innovate. They don't focus on superlatives; they focus on effort—"Just Do It."

Effective brand storytellers don't shy away from vulnerability, flaws, and failure. Yes, failure. Think about your favorite movies or novels. How many times does your hero fail? Frequently! We don't mind them failing. We expect them to fail. Then we expect them to get up off the ground and continue the quest. We want our hero to devour that failure and come back stronger, smarter, and more determined than ever.

Businesses are the same. When I chat with business leaders, I ask them about past failures, and they regale me with wonderful tales of missteps and awful ideas. When I hear the stories, I can relate to their setbacks and want to help them even more.

We know that every business has struggles. So why pretend anything different? If you have a well-known setback, shine a light on it. Turn it into a positive. Be like Ben & Jerry's® ice cream. Yes, they have a host of wildly successful

---

[100] https://www.aerogrammestudio.com/2013/03/07/pixars-22-rules-of-storytelling/

flavors, but they also have flops such as Rainforest Crunch, Mississippi Mud (made with Jack Daniels), and the infamous Schweddy Balls, named after the *Saturday Night Live* sketch. That one didn't go over so well in the more straitlaced parts of the country.

Ben & Jerry's didn't try to bury the duds with excuses and explanations. They buried them in the ground. Literally. It created a Flavor Graveyard at their Vermont headquarters and gave each of the deceased ice creams headstones. A sign proudly proclaims, "Celebrating our Failures since 1978." More than 300,000 visitors pay their respects annually.

FOCUS ON THE HEART OF YOUR STORY

Your story isn't your PR. Traditional PR tries to reach people with positive spins, facts, and information. It strives to make an intellectual argument. Your company story is much deeper than that. It's that personal connection between you and your employees, supporters, and customers. It's connecting through common emotion.

Don't get me wrong. I still think there's a time and a place for traditional PR. I just think businesses can experience deeper, more meaningful, longer lasting communication and connection simply by telling their story, being human instead of acting like a robo-company and being unafraid to express emotion.

This is especially true today, as traditional media venues (newspapers, magazines, television) shrink in scope, placing a greater onus on companies to tell their own stories. The days of sending out a press release and reading media coverage in the morning newspapers are over. Today, every company is a communications company.

Fortunately, there's a powerful and growing arsenal of storytelling tools and outlets. Websites, apps, blogs, social media, podcasts, YouTube channels, books and e-books, and even texts allow companies to reach consumers instantly. But how do you best cut through the clutter? By having a heart.

I pen a blog for our website, www.collaboration-llc.com. A few years ago, I wrote an essay called, "Is it Okay to Bring Your Heart to Work?"[101] I received more responses from that post than any I have ever written.

Part of what I wrote was, "Being relationship-centered as a business seems like common sense but is often not a priority for many leaders or organizations. Relationship-centered management requires leaders to be real with themselves and to truly care about those they lead. It requires a higher level of authenticity, transparency, and connectedness than most people are willing to express."

I know this goes against old-school business management consulting. Times have changed. People have changed. Employees and consumers increasingly tune out platitudes and superlatives that constituted marketing in the past. All the BS makes us gravitate to companies, causes, and individuals that come across as real. As human.

There's a company in San Luis Obispo called Meathead Movers. I love the name. They're poking a bit of fun at themselves, though the name also cleverly suggests they're strong, reliable, and probably cheap. But it isn't the name I most admire about the company, it's a stand they took in the community.

---

[101] https://collaboration-llc.com/is-it-okay-to-bring-your-heart-into-work/

Several years ago, Meathead Movers uncovered a troubling fact. Some of their moves involved women escaping domestic violence situations. These victims needed to flee immediately and worried about their abusers causing trouble. One move turned confrontational after the abuser showed up at the house. "I remember the conversations pretty vividly and feeling a tremendous amount of panic and sadness," recalled founder Aaron Steed.[102] "Handling those phone calls made it very real very quick."

The brothers decided they needed to do something. Don't worry, they advised the women. We'll take care of everything. For no charge. And we'll send our biggest, toughest movers to boot. They started to work in coordination with domestic violence shelters, providing victims with free moving services at all their locations in California.

Most companies would've made a big deal about this. "Look at us and all the good we're doing." Meathead Movers did not. It focused on spreading the word to those in need. The policy wasn't a PR stunt. It was part of their ethos, their culture. Employees felt good about the mission—that they were helping to address a pressing community need.

It wasn't until years later that word spread to the greater media. *Los Angeles Weekly* and *Huffington Post* ran articles. *The Today Show* and CNN followed up with reports of their own. The brothers decided to use the publicity to help encourage other moving companies around the country to offer similar support. They created a nonprofit and invited

---

[102] https://www.latimes.com/socal/daily-pilot/tn-wknd-et-1206-meathead-movers-20151206-story.html

others to join the effort. So far, several hundred businesses have donated services and products to aid victims.

"We've done hundreds of these moves, and it's a wonderful thing, I think, for our employees to feel," said Steed.[103] "We believe it saves lives, and it hopefully sets a trajectory for the young men and women to incorporate philanthropy into their life and to feel empowered that they can do something even if you're just a mover."

CRAFT AND TELL YOUR STORY

Why is your story important? Let's start with the fact that we're all story addicts. It's how we see the world. This addiction is a result of both nurture and nature. Our parents told us stories to get us to behave a certain way: Be nice so that Santa Claus will visit the house on Christmas. Get good grades to maximize your opportunities ahead. They also read us stories or showed us movies that followed a similar format: an ordinary hero thrust into an extraordinary challenge. Through hard work and creativity our hero achieves his goal. He slays the dragon, finds the gold, destroys the Death Star. The stories almost always had a positive ending, and we grew to crave those resolutions.

So we've been raised on a steady stream of stories, but our addiction goes beyond that. Our brains emit certain chemicals when they hear stories, whether we want them to or not.

The first is cortisol. This chemical is often released when we hear conflict. Cortisol makes us more likely to engage,

---

[103] Duerr, "They Help Women Move—Literally—Out of Abusive Relationships," PARA #4.

to act. We hear an argument brewing and snap into attention. Our brains are asking, do I need to act here? Am I in danger? That's why most stories start with conflict. It's a great way to engage the brain. It's the hook.

The next chemical is oxytocin, a compound that boosts our empathy and trust, like we discussed in the last chapter. Want a good dose of oxytocin? Listen to a baby laughing. Or crying. Our brains constantly scan for heroes and villains. Who can we trust? Who can we rally behind? Babies are a natural ally. When we see a baby in distress, we furrow our brow and want to help alleviate the problem.

Finally, if the story has a happy or otherwise satisfying ending, our brains release dopamine. Think of all the times we've watched a movie knowing the guy will get the girl or the cop will arrest the criminal, and still we get a rush when it happens. We even get a dopamine boost just thinking about the resolution.

Knowing all this, knowing that we are story animals, we are moved far more by story than data or facts, and that we tend to see everything—including our businesses—as part of a giant story, how do most companies communicate? By doing the exact opposite! Instead of giving us challenge-resolution, they give us superlatives: "Our products and services are the best!" "We do everything well! For a super low cost!" "Save BIG! Act now!"

"But I don't think I have a compelling story to tell," clients tell me. Of course you do. Your story is why you're in business in the first place. Starting a business is an epic task. Your story is about the challenges you and your team have had to overcome to continue the journey.

Start with your conflict, your initial challenge. What is your mission? Let people in on your quest. Maybe you started a restaurant because you believe a quality meal doesn't have to be expensive. That's your "why."

Then talk about the steps you're taking to fulfill the quest. This is the middle part of your story and can include the tests and challenges to the mission. It's also where you broaden your story to include the allies in your journey. Once you decided to start the restaurant, you enlisted local farmers to provide fresh ingredients and convinced an expert chef to join the cause. That's your "how."

Your resolution is the product or service your business currently offers. What have you and your team learned along the way? How have you changed? What can customers expect when they come to eat at your restaurant? That's your "what."

Once you hammer out your story, you can use it everywhere—from everyday conversations, to your About Us section on your website, to your sales pitches and presentations. A core story can fuel your social media and marketing efforts as well as strengthen your community relations and customer service.

I know it's hard for entrepreneurs and business leaders to make the shift from traditional PR to more heartfelt brand storytelling. They look around and see others clinging to the traditional ways of communicating. The key is to start small. Take baby steps. Once you start using storytelling, you won't want to stop. It's like writing from the heart for the first time. After that, everything else rings hollow.

Begin with a storytelling analysis of your materials and efforts to-date. See where you can substitute honest storytelling for industry jargon and PR spin.

Next, conduct a simple story-gathering effort. Ask your employees to share their best company-related stories. In my experience, the most compelling stories frequently come from unlikely sources or as afterthoughts.

Then write out a one-page narrative. Pen a simple version of your company story as a fiction writer would. Make up an ending, a glorious one. Who knows? It might just come true.

Finally, formulate a plan for how to use your stories. Start with something simple like authoring a new About Us section or rewriting your bio to make it less corporate and more human. Begin from there and expand. Test your story out. Find out which elements resonate the most with others, then build on those themes.

Above all, have a heart.

SUMMARY POINTS

- Just as your management style needs to evolve from "me" to "we," so does the story you tell about your company. Collaborative business leaders make the company and the mission the hero, not themselves.
- The best brand storytellers use proven literary techniques and embrace challenges, setbacks, and the full range of human emotion. They eliminate jargon and over-the-top PR ("World's Greatest!"), communicate like they would to a friend, and try to reach people through the heart as well as the head.
- To make the shift, start with a company-wide story-gathering effort and an analysis of marketing materials to-date. Next, pen a one-page narrative about the past, present, and future of your company. Test out the story to see which parts resonate the most. Then begin telling your story through your website, social media, and in person.
- Know that nobody is rooting for your company. They cheer for the story behind your company.

Visit Collaboration-LLC.com for a whitepaper titled, "How to Empower Your Team to Succeed Using the Freedom Scale."

E-MYTH BUSTING

E-Myth: Most successful entrepreneurs
are expert prognosticators.
E-Reality: Most successful entrepreneurs
are just plain lucky.

Microsoft CEO Steve Ballmer confidently predicted, "There's no chance that the iPhone is going to get any significant market share."[104] YouTube cofounder Steve Chen was pessimistic about the company's long-term viability, worrying aloud that "There's just not that many videos I want to watch."[105]

Entrepreneurs misreading the future is nothing new. Thomas Edison once declared, "Fooling around with the alternating current (AC) is just a waste of time. Nobody will use it, ever."[106]

Corner a successful entrepreneur at a bar and ask her how she did it. She'll probably toss out a few standard catchphrases like "demographic trends" or "market projections." Give her a couple drinks and you'll hear a more truthful answer: "luck."

---

[104] https://www.businessinsider.com/heres-what-steve-ballmer-thought-about-the-iphone-five-years-ago-2012
[105] https://www.telegraph.co.uk/technology/0/worst-tech-predictions-of-all-time/youtube-founders/.
[106] https://www.goodreads.com/quotes/3051240-fooling-around-with-alternating-current-is-just-a-waste-of.

All the successful startups have a good dose of it, far more than their PR staffs care to admit. You can have the right product, at the right time, in the perfect market, for the ideal price. ...and still go bankrupt. Maybe Apple decided to venture into your business sector. Or an unemployed lawyer opted to file a lawsuit against you because he can think of nothing better to do.

In business, luck counts. A lot. Have that horseshoe handy.

·

CHAPTER 9

HELD UP ON ACCOUNTABILITY

Here's a scenario I experience dozens of times a year: A CEO comes to my office to talk about her business. She's frustrated because growth has stalled despite her best efforts. She's tried putting in more hours, broadening the company's scope of business, and handing out raises. Nothing has worked.

She thinks it's a communication issue. She complains that her employees "don't get it," but admits she may be part of the problem and believes communication is a "two-way street." She's open to suggestions to improve things and get her company out of neutral and into high gear.

Before she continues her plea, I tell her communication is probably not the main issue. Then I commend her. "Any business leader who takes the time to talk about communication, to worry about communication, is probably a better communicator than he or she thinks."

I then ask her a series of questions to pinpoint the problem: "Do you give your employees specific benchmarks? How do you measure their success? If they fall short, what are the consequences?"

The CEO will usually say there are concrete expectations and measurables for her employees, but when we dig down, we usually see that these benchmarks are soft, ever-changing, and often unspoken. There's little follow-up and few ramifications when employees don't do their jobs.

"Your problem isn't communication," I tell the CEO. "It's accountability."

The CEO is well-intended, good-natured, and hard-working. She cares about her employees and wants to see them succeed. She talks with them frequently and assumes she is giving them everything they need. But she's missing a crucial ingredient: a consistent, fair, rewarding system of accountability.

Poor communication is the number one reason people contact our firm. Accountability is the number one problem we diagnose. That's not a shock. If lack of accountability was a disease, the American business community would be quarantined by now. The problem is an epidemic.

"One Out of Every Two Managers is Terrible at Accountability," concluded a *Harvard Business Review* study.[107] "… by far and away the single-most shirked responsibility of executives is holding people accountable. No matter how tough a game they may talk about performance, when it comes to holding people's feet to the fire, leaders step back from the heat."

---

[107] https://hbr.org/2012/11/one-out-of-every-two-managers-is-terrible-at-accountability

One out of two? In my experience, the number is even higher.

Several years ago, a CEO hired me to help with his cosmetic container company. He invited me to lunch with the lead salesperson. I knew little about the company but hoped to learn more during our meeting. So I started asking basic questions such as, "How do you target sales, cultivate leads, or share information with your sales team?" The salesperson struggled to answer each query and became defensive. Within minutes I knew accountability was a major problem at the company. The CEO did too. The salesperson sensed his days of coasting by would soon come to an end. He resigned the next day.

I wasn't surprised. We've experienced an accountability crisis over the last several decades, not just in our businesses but throughout society at large. Our politicians, celebrities, and community leaders refuse to admit wrongdoing even when everyone around them knows it. "Deny, deny, deny" has become de rigueur.

Even when our business leaders are clearly in the wrong and forced to give an apology, they still can't manage to do it. Instead, they issue these mealy-mouthed, accusatory, obfuscating, non-apology apologies. They say they're sorry "if there was any misunderstanding," implying the offended parties were too dumb to understand. They stress the company actions "do not reflect our company as a whole," even though they're company actions. They cast doubt on the accusers and attempt to play the victim. After the British Petroleum oil spill in 2010, a disaster that killed 11 drilling rig workers and spewed nearly five million barrels of oil into the Gulf of Mexico, BP chief executive Tony Hayward said, "There's no one who wants this over more than I do. I'd like my life back." He later apologized for the non-apology.

Is it any wonder that today's business leaders and employees see these examples and act accordingly? Of course not.

Beginning in the 1980s, a growing number of managers and entrepreneurs began to value popularity as much as success. They wanted to be liked. No, loved! They thought their employees couldn't handle criticism or being singled out. These are the same people who received trophies just for being on the team, they reasoned. An unkind word would crush them. Far better to focus on the positive.

At the same time, company priorities shifted away from individual results to group output. Companies used to hang sales boards in offices, allowing everyone to see who was contributing the most…and the least. The boards came down in the '80s and '90s as business leaders embraced a more touchy-feely approach, not wanting to hurt feelings.

I get it. The boards could be harsh, but the pendulum swung back too far. What happened after the shift in management style? Lackluster employees were able to hide among their more productive counterparts, angering the good workers and prompting many to leave the company. Managers struggled to pinpoint problem areas and underperforming employees. They became more hesitant to dish out constructive criticism or call workers out for failures. The whole thing became a giant, amorphous, feel-good glob of awfulness.

The psychology and rationale behind the shift couldn't have been more wrong. Contrary to popular stereotypes, employees actually want to know their standing, especially the productive ones—those you need to retain.

This includes millennials and Gen Y employees. They're tired of all the participation trophies. They're sick of covering for lesser workers. They crave a merit-based system. Or they wish to be told when their efforts are off base. They want accountability and they want to be held accountable.

Managers too are frustrated by the current system. They want to be able to know precisely which employees are cutting it and which ones need to be cut loose. Many of the business leaders we counsel have grown to be conflict averse. But with a little training and experience, they see the benefits of dealing with employees directly and honestly. They see that their employees need it and, contrary to public opinion, actually like it. Once they taste accountability, they don't want to return to the old ways.

Entrepreneurs are the worst of all. In getting that business off the ground, they're accountable to no one. They believe investors who lend them money are lucky to support their genius and will be rewarded in spades. Consumers who complain about a product "just don't get it." Entrepreneurs experience just enough success without accountability to convince themselves they'll never need it.

Most entrepreneurs I've counseled also tend to see accountability in black and white. Employees are either doing their job or they're not; they should either be praised or fired.

Collaborative leaders, I tell them, embrace the full spectrum of responsibility. They understand that each employee is unique and that each one responds to different methods. So they embrace a variety of steps, tactics, and approaches to instill accountability throughout their business.

When an employee doesn't perform, many entrepreneurs tend to conclude the worker has a personal flaw. He's too lazy, not dedicated enough, not smart enough, or in over his head.

Successful, collaborative leaders first examine the worker's skills, the office's processes, and the strategies that combine the two. Is the worker lazy, or does he not always know what's expected of him?

Entrepreneurs see themselves as bosses (as crusaders!) to be followed. If an employee can't hack it, hire someone else. Collaborative leaders see themselves as coaches for teaching and developing a competent team around them, one that can thrive in any situation.

Entrepreneurs tend to start their businesses with a group of close friends or relatives. They have a hard time shifting from friend-mode to manager-mode, even when the situation begs for it. Collaborative leaders strive to hire the best people available. Period.

Entrepreneurs see accountability as a problem for employees. It's a simple concept to them: "Just do your job." Collaborative business leaders see that accountability is a necessity for all levels of the company, starting at the top. They know actions speak louder than words. If managers offer excuses or blame others for shortcomings, workers will likely do the same.

Say a sales manager promises to follow up on a hot lead by the end of the week. Time is of the essence here. But the sales manager gets caught up in other business and tells the boss he'll get to it the following week. The boss says, okay, but "please jump on this as soon as possible." A poor manager will grumble that his sales staff is dropping the ball. The better manager will see that he is enabling his staff to do so.

When most entrepreneurs hire managers, they abdicate responsibility, especially in areas that aren't their specialty. They brag about it to the rest of the office: "Thank goodness we hired a new finance officer. Now I can get back to innovating!"

Collaborative business leaders understand the difference between abdication and delegation. They realize blind trust isn't lasting trust. They know they must still be involved at some level: "Thank goodness we hired a new finance officer. Now we can improve our modeling and get a better handle on revenues and expenditures."

Without accountability, there's no sustainability for your business. There's no chance of growth. There's no future.

Based on the hundreds of cases I've seen accountability fails tend to fall into several categories:

Undefined Expectations

I've talked to your employees. Thousands of them. Trust me, they don't have a clear idea of exactly what you expect of them. Oh, they know the generalities, the broad strokes. They get that they're supposed to handle a specified function, but they get confused when it comes to the specifics of the function. They could use a little clarity from you. Make that a lot.

Do you have a written list of tasks you wish them to complete? Are they ranked in order of importance? Is their focus ever supposed to change and, if so, when? Do you meet regularly to confirm expectations? Do you reward or reprimand employees when they don't meet expectations?

In most of the cases I see, the problem starts with the manager, not the employee. Business leaders simply don't spend enough time thinking about accountability, writing things down, expressing those expectations to workers, being consistent, and being accountable themselves.

Let's say you're the manager of a fitness club and you hire a new trainer. The woman comes highly recommended from another gym. She's been a successful trainer for years. You had a trainer leave, and the new employee takes over the current clients. Great job, you tell yourself. You filled an important opening with a quality worker. Now you can focus on other things.

After a few weeks, you notice your clients aren't renewing their training sessions at the same rate as before. Nobody has complained about the new trainer, but she now has several gaps in her schedule each day. You know turnover is inevitable, so you cut her some slack. But the dropout rate increases over the coming months and now you're seeing a real impact on company profits.

Before you criticize your new trainer, take a good look at yourself. Were you crystal clear in expressing your expectations to her? In writing? Was the goal just to train current clients or also to retain them as members of the gym? Did you want the new trainer to spend time learning clients' likes and dislikes, or did you just want her to jump in and start training the way she did at the old gym? If you expected turnover, did you tell your new trainer that you wanted her to focus on recruiting new members?

The more detailed and direct you can be with your expectations, the better your employees will be with their performance. Put another way, every time you're vague or wishy-washy with directions, you're not only handicapping your employee, but also harming your business and yourself.

Lack of Feedback

Managers typically give the most amount of guidance during the early stages of employment, then drop off quickly from there. It's a deluge of information during those first weeks, then a trickle of feedback from then on. Employees need a steady stream of feedback. And so do managers.

Take the fitness club example. Once you noticed clients weren't renewing, did you pick up the phone and ask them why? Maybe your new trainer is too tough. Or not tough enough. Maybe it's just bad luck. You won't know until you dig around.

Then did you have a conversation or two with your new trainer? Does she have any ideas as to why people aren't renewing? Any suggestions to rectify the situation? If you were specific with her at hiring that you wished for her to grow the practice by a specified amount, you should talk with her about how she's going to meet that expectation. More calls? Sign-up promotions? You can't be too specific.

This shouldn't be done by playing the blame game or voicing frustration. Practice positive accountability. Though her job is her responsibility, make sure she understands you're there to support her, that you want more than anything for her to succeed.

Many inexperienced managers see accountability from a negative point of view. "My employee isn't doing his job! He needs to be accountable!" Successful managers stress the positive side of accountability—credit, reward, advancement. When a company succeeds, they want everyone to feel they've played a role in that success.

Another important piece of feedback is this: Explain to your employees why you need them to perform a function. If you treat workers with a military-style, need-to-know approach, they're likely to question your purposes more often. Talk with them about the big picture and why they need to complete their tasks even if they don't immediately see the benefits.

Unspoken Expectations

The worst cases I see are managers who hire someone and then leave them alone to do their job. Too alone. Sometimes it's an employee in another location. Sometimes it's because they feel the employee doesn't need a lot of supervision. And sometimes managers claim they're just too busy to spend time reviewing and re-reviewing accountability. Make time. Face time. Supervise.

Entrepreneurs fail constantly at this. Many expect employees to be psychics who know exactly which tasks to perform and when. Sustainable businesses don't work this way. I've seen countless employees—bright, hard-working employees—who have no problem taking initiative, only to be reprimanded by a boss who keeps his expectations to himself. The result? A risk-averse staff that believes it's better to do nothing than to try to read a boss's mind.

Changing Expectations

Goals change. Focuses change. Every business experiences change. But as your company changes course, are you changing employee expectations without telling them? Constantly ask yourself, *"What do I want employee X to be doing today, tomorrow, and in the weeks ahead?"*

When the client drop-off rate at the gym began to severely impact the company's revenues, in your mind the situation probably shifted from a service issue to a service and sales issue. You know you need more bodies in the door. But does your new trainer know this? Or maybe, after a round of calls to clients, you've persuaded most clients to give the new trainer a second chance. Are you clear with her that your expectation is she'll do everything possible to keep them happy and signed up at the gym?

Lack of Timelines

Businesses abide by strict timelines. They need to make a certain amount of revenue to cover payroll, produce a product, and make rent. They all operate according to timelines, yet when it comes to employees, they get lenient. They excuse missed deadlines. Then they tend to overcompensate and insist on unreachable timelines. Why are companies so afraid of employee timelines?

It's far better to establish a workable timeline from the beginning. Talk with that employee about what you can expect from her in a month, six months, or a year. Start conservatively, then revisit timelines throughout the year. Are there any developments, either internal or external, that could impact those timelines? Does the employee feel the timelines need adjusting?

Again, the more specific the better—for the employee and everyone else. It's like raising money. You'll be far more successful with a specific amount for a specific purpose and a giant fundraising thermometer on the wall that allows everyone to see the progress. Trust me, your employees want measurables and timelines. They want to know when they're fulfilling your expectations and when they're falling short.

Conflict Aversion

We've grown resistant to conflict in the workplace (and in life) over the last several decades. When it comes to even the smallest disagreement, we're wimps, wusses, milksops. We've forgotten that disagreement is fine, necessary even, for a company (or a relationship) to thrive. We're human. We're going to disagree. Do we embrace that fact, or do we run from it?

In the workplace, we tend to run. We ignore and gloss over. We've even created a new language, words and phrases designed not to offend at any cost. Instead of asking direct questions like "Did you close the sale this morning?" we say things like, "Just checking in" or "Any updates to share?" Instead of giving direct feedback, we tell colleagues their work "Looks great!" when it's mediocre or "You may want to tweak it a bit" when a complete overhaul is needed.

Of course, as any psychologist will tell you, conflict aversion doesn't make conflict go away. It has the opposite impact. It allows feelings to simmer and grow, usually resulting in much more harm.

Imagine that employee who has heard nothing but phony praise for his lackluster work since day one at the company. He thinks he's doing a wonderful job. When you bring him into the office and say, "I'm sorry but we're going to have to let you go" (instead of "You're being fired"), he's dumb-founded. What about all the attaboy emails? What about all the exclamation points you used with your positive feedback?

There's a common perception that bosses need to be especially conflict avoidant with millennials and Gen Z employees. Ignore that perception; it's just not true. I have talked with hundreds of them. They need you to be direct with them. They want you to be direct with them. The company needs you to be direct with them. They can handle it, and so can you.

Lack of Tact

The flip side of conflict avoidance is the manager who is too blunt. These types tend to say nothing for extended periods, then lash out at their employees. That's not a sustainable relationship. Accountability means steady contact and support, honest feedback, and tact.

See yourself as a coach. Some employees need to be told something only once to force a change, while others need more feedback. Some fuel on praise, while others love a challenge.

One productive way to deal with your employees in a respectful fashion is to place accountability in their hands. Review the goals for the job, the more detailed the better, then ask them how they plan to reach those objectives. Ask how you can best support them. "Do you want to do a weekly meeting or regular updates?" "Can you handle this alone, or do you need some help?" "How do you plan to keep us apprised of your progress?"

Character vs. Competency

Too often, poor managers assume lack of accountability is rooted in character flaws. If employees fail to complete an important task, it's because they're unfocused, not 100% committed, or just plain lazy.

I hear the word "lazy" frequently. Most of the time, it's not accurate at all. When my colleagues and I do a deeper analysis of the company, we often find the "lazy" employee is a confused employee, an unprepared employee, or an employee who has no idea what he needs to do, when he needs to do it, and how he needs to update his superiors.

Author Stephen M. R. Covey talks about this in his book *The Speed of Trust*.[108] To build trust and strengthen accountability, he encourages business leaders to see their employees as a tree. The top part of the tree is competence, representing their record of success and the skills they've gained. The roots of the tree are character, representing their intentions and motivations for the job.

When employees fail to perform, inexperienced managers go straight to the roots of the tree—character. They tell themselves the problem is the result of a personality flaw: The employees don't care. They're lazy.

Covey stresses the importance of first looking to the top of the tree—competency and capability—before assuming employees are lazy or have some other character shortcoming. Have you clearly spelled out what they need to do and when they need to do it? Have you provided them with the necessary training? Do you meet regularly to support them?

---

[108] Stephen M. R. Covey, *The Speed of Trust* (Free Press, 2006).

Then, and only then, should you begin to look at character issues.

Look, there's a reason why you hired these employees. They possessed skills and experiences you valued, wowed you during an interview, or came to you highly recommended from people you respect. Cut them some slack when it comes to questioning their character. Perhaps they aren't the problem. Perhaps it's you.

Boss to the Rescue

Most business leaders I counsel are result-oriented. For the most part, that's a good thing. We should all be concerned with the bottom line, right?

Well, not always. Sometimes we should be more concerned with long-term success.

When employees fail to complete a job, managers have several options. They can do nothing and hope the problem solves itself. Spoiler: it rarely does. Or they can jump in and solve the problem. "Don't worry, I got it." Many managers love this role. They get to play superhero, coming to the rescue at the last minute to save the day.

But what happens after the manager "solves" the problem? Do the employees grow and benefit? No. Are they better able to handle similar issues in the future? No. Are they going to take more initiative? Probably not.

"Savior" bosses don't realize it, but they cause more problems than they solve. I've seen several companies where bosses jump in so often, employees purposely set the stage for them to do so. That approach may be great for a boss's ego, but it's ominous for the company's future.

A third approach is to call employees in, review the situation in detail, then help them fashion a solution they can implement. Save the superhero cape for another day.

Defensiveness

The lack of accountability at a business is like a disease that attacks a tree. You might not notice it at first, but the damage is being inflicted every day. Sometimes, by the time you realize you have a serious illness, the destruction is irreparable.

The problem with an unclear, inconsistent system of accountability is that both sides—employees and managers—tend to get settled into their opinions as to who's responsible. They point fingers. They blame. They get defensive and refuse to budge in their views or approaches. And the problems multiply.

I've gone to companies where the two sides could barely sit in a room together, let alone work together. They come in with arms crossed and a detailed account of why everything they've done is right and good for the company; it's the others who are to blame.

That's the time to get the entire concept of blame out of the room. There's no such thing as blame, I tell them. Blame is unmeasurable and unhelpful. There are only successes and setbacks. Good companies share equally in both.

The Software Panacea

Another situation I see all too frequently is the company that decides software programs can solve accountability challenges. "If we install this new system, everyone will know what to do and be held accountable accordingly." If only it was that easy.

Accountability problems are usually relationship problems. And no relationship is going to get fixed by a computer. Sure, software programs can help provide all sides with useful information. But they're not going to be able to explain the "why" behind that information.

No, instilling an accountable culture is going to take time, effort, and your best relationship skills. It's well worth it. Increased accountability = immediate returns. I've seen companies experience double-digit growth within days after they implement a new system of accountability. It's an investment with quick, guaranteed returns. Here's how to get started:

STEPS TO ESTABLISH ACCOUNTABILITY

1. Do an analysis. Better yet, hire a firm to do so. This can be done in relatively short order. You just need to diagnose where your business comes up short in accountability.

2. Next, it's pow-wow time. With every party. I try to keep these meetings on general terms to begin, then gradually get more specific. If the employees are salespeople, talk about how they feel things are going. Are they clear on their goals and how they should be spending their days? What are the biggest challenges? The largest potential areas of growth? Do they feel supported? What else can you and others do to help? Try not to make these meetings confrontational. The last thing you want is for your employees to feel they're on trial. Instead, seek to enlist them as partners to solve particular challenges. Give them more insight and information than they normally receive.

"We are trying to pass our top competitor by the end of the year." "We have an interested buyer, but we need to boost sales by 10 percent this quarter."

3. After you've had a good give-and-take or two, work together to create desired outcomes for the employees. The more detailed the better. Don't just say, "I want you to increase sales by 10 percent this quarter." Work collaboratively to agree on a plan that specifies the who, what, when, where, and how of reaching that goal.

4. At the same time, come up with a plan in case employees come up short. Put it on them: "How should I best hold you accountable?" You'd be surprised how many employees crave this. They want consequences because they know consequences will spur them to act.

5. Then create a follow-up process. This can be in-person meetings, phone calls, computer communications, work management programs such as Asana®, or a combination of all four. The important point here is to get something down in writing—objectives and measurables that all sides can see and agree to. Many companies have a professional who's responsible for follow-up. This is a wise move because follow-up is crucial for establishing accountability. Managers should ask themselves, "Who is doing follow-up at my company?" Is it one person? Multiple people? Or maybe it's no one at all.

6. Once everything is in place, clear time to revisit the system on a regular basis. Perhaps a change in the economy makes sales goals unrealistic. Or maybe your sales team is doing so well that it's time to hire more people. Accountability systems are like grand pianos—they work

great and are pleasing to all…as long as they're regularly fine-tuned.

Entrepreneurs especially struggle with accountability. They tend to have crazy high expectations for hirees. They don't understand industry norms or proven ways to manage people. They toss goals around like confetti. Then they're upset when workers don't meet their arbitrary expectations. It's a recipe for disaster.

What's key here is a mind shift. Entrepreneurs are focused on their individual goals for the company. That can't be sustained. They need to change their way of thinking from "me" to "we." Yes, establishing accountability systems is going to take some time and will probably toss a little cold water on unrealistic goals. But entrepreneurs need to put their egos aside and understand that they're doing things to benefit the entire team, not just themselves.

Entrepreneurs must be held to accountability systems as well, letting their actions speak louder than their words. If they require their staff to keep an accounting of their hours, then they should keep an accounting of their hours as well. And when they fail to meet expectations, they should be honest with their workers. Share the shortcomings as well as plans to correct them. Walk the walk.

Companies that fail on the accountability front are destined to fail overall. Unless they implement accountability systems, it's only a matter of time before they're out of business.

We can see corporate accountability fails even from the outside. If a restaurant you frequent has a dish that varies in quality each time you order it, there's a failure of accountability. If you experience different levels of help and politeness each time you call the same utility, I guarantee you there's a failure of accountability going on inside that company. If an outsider can sense it's a problem, it's a problem.

SUMMARY POINTS

- Though communication is the number one reason business leaders contact our firm, accountability is the number one problem we diagnose. Studies show half of all business managers are "terrible" at accountability.

- Accountability problems tend to fall into several different categories: undefined, unspoken, or changing expectations; a lack of feedback or timelines; conflict aversion; tactless behavior; character versus competency; boss-to-the-rescue syndrome; defensiveness; or believing software is a cure-all.

- Our approach to helping companies with accountability starts with a deep dive analysis to better understand where things are breaking down. We then facilitate a series of collaborative meetings to produce mutually agreed upon goals and processes.

- Instead of a one-size-fits-all approach, ask employees how they wish to be held accountable. Together, craft an achievable follow-up process and agree to revisit the issues regularly. You'll be surprised how much employees crave detailed and consistent accountability.

Visit Collaboration-LLC.com for a whitepaper titled, "Maintaining Sustainable Profitability."

E-MYTH BUSTING

E-Myth: Most entrepreneurs are young and tech-savvy.
E-Reality: Most entrepreneurs are older and tech-challenged.

The young, high-tech entrepreneurs are better at one thing: grabbing the spotlight so often that we tend to see them as the entrepreneurial prototype. Time to look again. The entrepreneurial world is much grayer and less wired than conventional wisdom would have you believe.

More than half of all startups are initiated by entrepreneurs over the age of 50. For most, the startup is a second (or third, fourth, fifth) career, an idea they've been wanting to pursue for decades. Only 16 percent of all new companies are started by people under 35.[109]

And the vast majority of all startups are in businesses outside the tech world. Silicon Valley might draw the most amount of attention, and VC funding, but most entrepreneurial activity takes place on Main Street or in home offices.

---

[109] https://smallbiztrends.com/2016/11/startup-statistics-small-business.html

> **E-Myth: Many successful entrepreneurs
> are college dropouts.
> E-Reality: Stay in school.**

Teenagers trying to avoid college will frequently drop the name of Bill Gates, Steve Jobs, or a handful of other business leaders who dropped out of school and then went on to entrepreneurial riches. If your teenager tries that out on you, calmly reply that 95 percent of all entrepreneurs have at least a bachelor's degree.[110]

Then hit him with stories about successful entrepreneurs who found their future business partners while at a university. Google cofounders Sergey Brin and Larry Page, for example, met at Stanford graduate school. Take that, slacker!

You might also want to add that entrepreneurs have a much better chance of success if they start the business with a partner. Sorry, junior. It's school for you. Hit the books and start networking.

---

[110] https://www.inc.com/neil-patel/6-things-that-entrepreneurs-did-before-they-became-entrepreneurs.html

CHAPTER 10

HARD TO PROCESS

Click on a television profile about an entrepreneur. I guarantee you a prime focus will be on the beginnings of the business, that big "aha" moment when the entrepreneur experienced a stroke of genius for a new product or service. We love hearing about those moments, those lightning bolts of inspiration.

Nick Woodman, for example, wanted to take videos of himself surfing, so he founded GoPro®. Donald Fisher couldn't find jeans that fit, so he started The Gap®. Roommates Brian Chesky and Joe Gebbia struggled to pay their rent in San Francisco, so they purchased a couple of air mattresses, hosted a few guests, and started Airbnb®. Great stories. They leave us with the impression that successful businesses stem from magical moments. "Be open to opportunity," they suggest. Lightning can strike any time.

That's what Adora Cheung and her brother Aaron believed. Their "aha" moment came from an unlikely source—Aaron's smelly clothes and dirty dishes. Adora enjoyed sharing an apartment with her brother, but his cleaning skills left a lot to be desired. After much urging from his sister, Aaron relented to the idea of hiring a cleaning service to tidy up their residence.[111]

What they discovered was a wholly inefficient and outdated market. They called numerous companies and learned they charged hundreds of dollars for a cleaning but only paid their cleaners minimum wage. The cleaning companies relied on archaic, labor-intensive management; they hand-scheduled appointments and took payments in person or over the phone. At the same time, they didn't screen cleaners for professional or criminal backgrounds. Call today and a felon could be mopping your floors in no time!

The Cheungs thought there was a better approach, a way to cut out the middleman, digitize management, screen cleaners, reduce costs, and improve overall efficiency. They wanted to upend the house cleaning market the way Uber changed ride sharing or how Airbnb revolutionized the hospitality industry. Deciding to pair individual contractors with consumers who desired a house cleaning through an easy-to-use website and phone app platform, they called the venture Homejoy™.

The Cheungs' "aha" moment made all kinds of sense. House cleaning is a $400 billion industry that is ripe for a "gig economy" makeover ala Uber or Airbnb. There's proven demand and solid models for reform. Venture capitalists

---

[111] https://www.wired.com/2015/10/why-homejoy-failed/.

jumped on board to the tune of $40 million for the Cheungs to launch Homejoy.[112] The media fawned.

A look behind the scenes revealed less tidy quarters, starting with the fact that the Cheungs, two computer engineers, knew nothing about cleaning a house. Fine, you say. Anyone can learn to do that in a day or two. Adora tried. She grabbed a mop and started to clean homes, educating herself about the best chemicals to use, ways to speed cleaning, and how to deal with customers.[113] Great, though if I'm one of her backers, I'd make sure Homejoy was well stocked with professionals who understood the cleaning business from all angles.

Homejoy started with a host of attention-grabbing deals, including a Groupon promotion for just $19.99 to clean a whole apartment. Consumers gobbled it up, swamping the company with appointment requests. Homejoy struggled to keep up. The resulting consumer reviews were unkind. Users liked the price but complained about the quality of service and last-minute cancellations. Most took advantage of the introductory discounts, then never used the service again. Homejoy managed to retain just 10 percent of its customers.[114] Yikes.

Meanwhile, the company faced several lawsuits from contractors who argued that they weren't contractors at all (like Uber drivers) but full-time employees due to the number of hours they were required to work. Backers began getting nervous, pulling back on their investments. Hemorrhaging

---

[112] https://www.wired.com/2015/10/why-homejoy-failed/

[113] https://wpcurve.com/homejoy-adora-cheung/

[114] https://www.wired.com/2015/10/why-homejoy-failed/

money and staring at mounting legal costs, Homejoy shuttered just two years after opening. Adora Cheung pointed to the court cases, saying they were the "deciding factor" in the decision to shut down.

But were they? Other contract-for-hire services, like Uber, faced similar legal challenges and overcame them, paving the way for similar "shared economy" businesses in all markets. Homejoy could've restructured hours and schedules to overcome this obstacle.

No, Homejoy lost its way thanks to a far bigger concern, one that frequently cripples growing businesses: failure to create a viable process.

Homejoy had no problem attracting customers (proof of a great idea), it just couldn't retain them (proof of poor execution and process). Why? Uneven service, for one. If customers would rather pay $100 for a spotless apartment than $20 for a mediocre cleaning, give them what they want. Introductory offers can be a good way to get people to try a service, but Homejoy should've (A) made sure those initial cleanings were damn good ones and (B) stopped giving away $20 cleanings after the first couple of months.

Homejoy also lost business when contractors simply arranged on their own to do private cleanings for users, cutting the company out of the mix. Homejoy failed to convince cleaning contractors of the long-term value of working together.

My partner Steve and I rent a back unit of our house from time to time through Airbnb. I've had multiple offers from Airbnb guests to rent the house outside the service. I always say no. To do so would jeopardize my standing at Airbnb, a consistent source of guests. Airbnb also helps with disputes and requires guests to pay for anything they damage. They provide significant value to both guests and hosts.

Homejoy never managed to do the same. The company could've instituted better insurance programs, for instance, ones that gave assurance to users and cleaners should any property be damaged. They could've set up a fair pricing schedule that paid cleaners amply, convinced consumers they were getting a good deal, and carved out a small fee for themselves on every transaction. They didn't.

But competitors like Handy did, picking up where Homejoy failed by implementing a solid process that resulted in consistent quality, ease of use, and, most importantly, sustainable profit. Handy is now in 37 locations, with more than 50,000 independent cleaners who give the company high ratings on Glassdoor.[115] The company pays above minimum wage and has now branched into furniture assembly through a partnership with Walmart.[116]

STRATEGY VS. EXECUTION

Process. The word alone causes many entrepreneurs and business leaders to yawn or flee the room. Process isn't sexy, in their minds. It's not innovative. It's not game changing. You can't get on the cover of a business magazine with process. You hear serial entrepreneurs talk about this all the time. "I'm an ideas guy," they'll say. "I just want to get this thing off the ground, then move on to another innovation."

---

[115] https //www.glassdoor.com/Overview/Working-at-Handy-EI_IE680570.11,16.htm

[116] https://techcrunch.com/2018/08/30/walmart-com-now-sells-handys-installation-and-assembly-services/

But how many times do we see an innovative product or a business get off the ground...then crash with a thud shortly thereafter? More interestingly, take a closer look and you'll see something surprising—nearly identical products and companies still thriving.

Jolt Cola, for instance, began with a bang in the mid-'80s, promising drinkers "all the sugar and twice the caffeine." They marketed their product like a novelty act, a soda for people proud to drink something unhealthy.[117] Parents, nutritionists, and the general public turned up their noses, and Jolt began a downward spiral until the company declared bankruptcy in 2009.[118] Dollar General is trying to revive the brand, with limited success. The cola has been banished to the dollar bin, literally and figuratively.

Meanwhile, Dietrich Mateschitz cofounded Red Bull at the same time Jolt Cola hit the market. Mateschitz, an Austrian consumer goods marketer, came up with the idea for an energy drink after tasting a sweet, syrupy beverage that gave him a boost while traveling in Thailand. He partnered with Thai businessman Chaleo Yoovidhya, perfected the formula, and started selling Red Bull in Europe.[119]

Red Bull and Jolt Cola are both basically cans of sugar water with high levels of caffeine. But Mateschitz took a much different sales approach. Instead of boasting about the beverage's unhealthiness, the company marketed Red Bull to

---

[117] http://adage.com/article/cmo-strategy/wake-america-jolt-cola-coming-back/310399/

[118] https://blogs.wsj.com/bankruptcy/2009/09/29/jolt-cola-looks-to-recharge-in-bankruptcy/

[119] https://www.nytimes.com/2012/03/19/business/chaleo-yoovidhya-dies-created-red-bull-energy-drink.html

athletes and adventurers, with special emphasis on extreme sports. They shrunk the can from 12 ounces to 8.4 ounces and sold it for three times the price of a soda. "It Gives You Wings," proclaimed Red Bull (at least until a judge ruled in a successful class action lawsuit that a can of Red Bull provides no more energy than a cup of coffee).[120]

Red Bull can afford the lawsuit. The company sold more than six billion cans of the stuff in 2017.[121] Smaller cans for three times the price of a Coke? Obviously there is a huge and growing market for highly caffeinated sugar water. Red Bull capitalized on that market. Jolt missed the boat.

From the beginning, Red Bull had not only a clear vision but, more importantly, a solid process to make that vision a reality. Red Bull would be the drink of choice for extreme athletes and those who admired them. So instead of purchasing expensive in-store placements or television advertising, the company sponsored motocross races and surf competitions.

More importantly, Mateschitz, a veteran global marketer at Unilever, made sure Red Bull was available in stores around the world. The marketing was brilliant, but the execution was even better. Red Bull spends pennies compared to giants Coca Cola® and Pepsi™, yet their products can be found in more than 170 countries around the world. That's a process!

Look at other companies that cratered while identical ones soared. Louis Borders (Borders Books) had a novel idea for a service that delivered groceries to the home. He persuaded

---

[120] https://www.nbcnews.com/business/consumer/red-bull-drinkers-can-claim-10-over-gives-you-wings-n221901

[121] https://energydrink-us.redbull.com/en/company

investors to kick in $375 million and launched Webvan in 1999. Wall Street swooned, boosting Webvan's stock to more than $1.2 billion.[122] We all love convenience, and we all shop for groceries, after all. Borders had a million-dollar idea and the backing to boot.

Problems surfaced immediately. Webvan agreed to construct $1 billion worth of warehouses in 26 cities instead of testing the service in a city or two. Consumers showed interest at first but decided they would rather pick out their own groceries. Webvan closed its doors two years after its IPO.

A year later, FreshDirect® opened a nearly identical operation, but focused on the greater New York City area. They started small, with an emphasis on speed and keeping products fresh, just like the name suggested. When consumers complained about excessive packaging, they trimmed the number of boxes needed for each shipment. They also streamlined their product offerings and cut order fulfillment times to keep the operation moving smoothly.

"We don't ship Evian to Oklahoma," FreshDirect Chief Executive Jason Ackerman told the *Wall Street Journal*. "We're not a national shipping business. We focus on being the best local food, fresh food retailer. And a lot of the tech is to support that."[123]

The company recently opened a state-of-the-art, 400,000 sq. ft. distribution facility and expanded its service to the Philadelphia and Washington, D.C., metro areas. They want

---

[122] https://www.forbes.com/sites/theyec/2014/09/18/surprising-lessons-from-companies-that-failed-despite-a-fail-proof-product/

[123] https://www.wsj.com/articles/inside-the-food-fight-over-home-delivery-1531906200

to continue growing, but at a pace their processes can handle. To capitalize on the concept, they know they need to be implementation experts, especially with a growing list of competitors that includes Amazon, Walmart, and large grocery chains such as Kroger.

Speaking of food, restaurants are the embodiment of the importance of process more than inspiration. Restaurateurs build gorgeous dining rooms and develop mouth-watering menus. People rave about their creativity, their talent, their taste. But how many of those chefs and restaurant owners are putting the same amount of time and effort into the process of running the restaurant once it's off the ground?

Guy Fieri, with his spiked platinum hair and unbridled enthusiasm for food, is one of America's most famous and popular chefs. While other celebrity chefs focus on five-star fare, Fieri turns his attention to blue-collar America. He promotes mom and pop eateries across the country as the TV host of *Diners, Drive-Ins and Dives*, while his successful restaurants serve up heaping plates of Mac Daddy Mac n' Cheese and Trash Can Nachos.[124]

America loves Fieri's brand of "comfort food gone wild."[125] So what better place to capitalize on that devotion than a giant, 500-seat restaurant in the heart of Times Square? Guy's American Kitchen and Bar opened for business in the fall of 2012.

Critics panned the establishment from the get-go. *The New York Times* penned a review so harsh it went viral,

---

[124] https://www.foodnetwork.com/profiles/talent/guy-fieri/guy-fieris-top-recipes

[125] https://www.nytimes.com/2017/12/29/dining/guy-fieri-restaurant-closing.html

giving the restaurant zero stars and asking such questions of Fieri as, "Were you struck by how very far from awesome the Awesome Pretzel Chicken Tenders are? If you hadn't come up with the recipe yourself, would you ever guess that the shiny tissue of breading that exudes grease onto the plate contains either pretzels or smoked almonds?"[126]

The reviews skewered Guy's American Kitchen and Bar, but they weren't the reason the restaurant failed. Indeed, patrons continued to pack the restaurant for the next five years, while Fieri's TV shows continued to help draw folks in.

What killed Guy's American Kitchen and Bar? Process. A few years after the opening, Fieri admitted his name might be on the door, but he never oversaw the meals or the operation. "Also, remember it's a licensing deal," he told *Las Vegas Weekly*. "I'm the chef, I make the recipes, I make the idea and I give it to a group. Let's be realistic about what this was."[127]

That's far from the message he gave *The Today Show* at the restaurant's opening, telling host Savannah Guthrie he had personally overseen the "painstaking" training process and restaurant setup. "This is more heart and soul," he bragged. "This is not just a name stamp."[128]

Plenty of big-name chefs license their name and brands. Fieri lends his image to dozens of ventures, from barbecue sauces and salsas, to pans and knives, to Guy's Burger

---

[126] https://www.nytimes.com/2012/11/14/dining/reviews/restaurant-review-guys-american-kitchen-bar-in-times-square.html

[127] https://lasvegasweekly.com/dining/chef-talk/2014/apr/16/talking-big-flavors-and-big-vegas-openings-guy-fie/.

[128] https://www.grubstreet.com/2012/11/guy-fieri-responds-to-restaurant-review.html.

Joint on Carnival Cruise Lines. Obviously, Fieri isn't the one mixing the salsas and flipping burgers at sea. The only way he can succeed is if he institutes and manages a quality-control process that ensures his standards are reflected in every venture that features his name.

Guy's American Kitchen and Grill didn't even come close. More damaging than reviews from *The New York Times* were the reviews on Yelp and Tripadvisor from customers who love Fieri and his take on food. They complained not just about the food but about long waits, mediocre service, unsanitary environments, and even instances of having to eat on the floor.[129] No restaurant, no matter how popular its chef, is going to survive that.

I've seen similar operational struggles at every startup I've counseled. This problem begins well before day one. It begins the minute the founders start dedicating a greater share of their attention to the concepts rather than the nuts and bolts of the business. According to a survey published in *Harvard Business Review*, only 8 percent of business leaders are good at both strategy and execution.[130]

HOW TO PRIORITIZE YOUR PROCESS

When I counsel clients struggling with process, the first thing I tell them is to get rid of the word itself. Change the terminology from words you find boring ("operations" or "execution," for example) to terms that excite you ("satisfaction levels,"

---

[129] https://www.nytimes.com/2012/11/14/dining/reviews/restaurant-review-guys-american-kitchen-bar-in-times-square.html.

[130] https://hbr.org/2015/12/only-8-of-leaders-are-good-at-both-strategy-and-execution

"growth rates," "gold stars!"). Most entrepreneurs and business leaders enjoy problem-solving. So reframe "execution" as "challenges in need of solutions."

One way I get stubborn business leaders to begin changing their mindsets is simply by asking, "So you're fine with being a small company?" "Of course not," they shoot back. "Well," I reply, "unless you adopt an entirely new approach and attitude surrounding your execution, the company is going to remain stagnant and small." They need to understand that if they're not 100 percent invested in and supportive of the process, nobody at the company will be. The manager sets the tone. Rolled eyes and skipped meetings will kill any process, no matter how well thought out it is.

Those conversations have one of two outcomes: the manager either tosses me out of the office...or agrees to take a fresh look at their process. Fortunately, I haven't been tossed from too many offices.

Next, we begin to examine the company's execution, starting from a micro point of view then branching out. How much time does the manager devote to process? As much as innovation or the other, sexier parts of the business? Is a time adjustment needed? An attitude change?

Then we move to the interaction with the rest of the team. This takes the form of both words and deeds. Managers need to make clear that the company is committed to execution. Be precise, I counsel them. "Our goal is 100% customer satisfaction and retention," for example. "We are shooting for a five-star Yelp rating." Make it a contest; make it fun. Highlight workers who excel at execution jobs that often go unnoticed—the employee who makes a service call on a weekend or the one who calmed an unhappy customer.

Through rewards, measurements and, most importantly, a manager's time and focus, demonstrate that execution is paramount.

You can tell from a phone call which companies emphasize this and which don't. Call Zappos to purchase a pair of shoes, for instance. Unlike other online retailers, they encourage phone calls. They put the 1-800 number in big letters on every page of the catalog and throughout the website. They'll take your call 24 hours a day and won't shuffle you off to different divisions. They'll answer your questions and process your order right away.

There are thousands of shoe businesses in America. Zappos offers a product you can get anywhere. Where they stand out from others in the field is in their execution. The company stresses that concept with every hire and trains each one to carry out the mission. Zappos emphasizes process innovation over product innovation.

Good process is a product of the corporate culture. It's the messages that stem from the top of the company, through all the employees, out to customers, and on to the public at large. Make sure your culture prioritizes process.

One way to do this is through a series of meetings with staff, conducted personally or organized by an outside professional. The goal of the meetings is to understand how the employees see the company mission, its values, and its priorities. You may think that employees know that, say, customer service is a top priority. But if you spend all your time talking about your next big idea (I'm looking at you, Elon Musk), your employees will act accordingly.

Next, make sure budgeting and staff allocation reflect your culture. Here is where most startups fail miserably.

How many times have you read the hoopla about a new product, plunked down some money, then struggled to figure out how it worked? The instructions are confusing, and you can't get ahold of anyone on the phone. You go to the website, but it only has a few answers to basic questions. You curse the company and vow never to buy something from them again.

This happens frequently because startups and young businesses fail to commit the resources necessary to ensure a viable process. Take a young software firm, for example. The founders have an idea for a new product that's going to wow the marketplace. They work like crazy to perfect it, then hire a few salespeople to start generating revenue. All the energy of the company is focused on bringing the product to market. The founders aren't focused on customer experience, consumer feedback, or team building. They just want to launch the concept and sell it to as many people as possible. They aren't allocating resources 50/50 between idea and execution. Far from it.

Most business leaders in this position also fail to distinguish between growth and smart growth. There's a huge difference. Growth is great...but only if the company can handle it. That's where a solid process comes into play. Scalability, agility, and sustainability are only possible with a sound process.

Even mature businesses make this mistake. Think of Krispy Kreme® or Zynga®. They attempted to scale too rapidly, failed miserably, then had to scale back operations and reestablish a new process to stay in business.

The problem is even more acute with startups and fledgling businesses. *Inc.* Magazine publishes an annual list of the 5,000 fastest growing companies. Entrepreneurs love to see their names on this list. It helps them raise money, boost sales, and elevate their profile.

But a follow-up study conducted by the Kauffman Foundation and *Inc.* Magazine concluded the vast majority of these fast-rising companies stumble after making the list. Specifically, "What they found was startling: about two-thirds of the companies that made the list had shrunk in size, gone out of business, or been disadvantageously sold. Why? Because they failed to make it through the fourth and final stage of enterprise maturity, where a company finally becomes self- sustaining."[131]

So the next issue we tackle with companies is the adaptability and the sustainability of the process. Every company starts out with a plan. Every successful company has had to change that plan, whether it be a little fine-tuning or a radical overhaul. The question we help companies answer is, "Your business has evolved, but has your process evolved as well?"

Many entrepreneurs fall into the trap of believing their products are perfect, that there is a market for them today, and that there will always be strong demand. Listen, stick-to-itiveness is essential during the initial stages of growth. Often, force of will is the only thing that can get a company up and running. But far too many entrepreneurs start believing their ideas and innovations are flawless. Their egos prevent them from seeing when the marketplace or their own employees have a different view. A solid process can act as an important ego check. It allows a company to better see and react to market realities.

---

[131] http://fortune.com/2016/03/07/fast-growth-companies-fail/

If the business has tasted success, I give the leaders a pat on the back and tell them, "Well done." But then I have a frank discussion with them about the feedback, whether from their staff, their customers, or the media. I try to get them to look at the situation as objectively as possible. What changes need to take place for the company to succeed in the future? How can we enhance the process to meet anticipated needs?

Another technique I employ here is scenario playing. How would the company fare if, say, it received a wave of negative publicity, or a competitor came to market with a far superior product? What short-term and long-term steps would you take? On the other hand, what would happen if your company landed a huge new piece of business? Could your staff handle it? You know the expression strive for the best, plan for the worst? Well, successful companies strive for the best, plan for the worst—and plan for the best.

It's crucial for business leaders to understand that processes need to grow in sophistication as the company matures. You want to create processes that can not only react to any new challenge or opportunity but anticipate them and guide staff on how to do their jobs proactively.

Finally, though I hesitate to go against *The Godfather*, Michael Corleone (Al Pacino) was wrong when he told his brother Sonny (James Caan), "It's not personal, Sonny. It's strictly business." All business is personal to a certain degree. No company has ever removed all egos and feelings from its operations.

The best way to guard against that is to get everyone at a company to buy into a specific set of measurables and benchmarks, ones that ensure process will be an equal partner to innovation. The objective is to avoid personal disagreements in the future as much as possible and ensure the decision-making is rational and fact driven. That's an offer no company can refuse.

SUMMARY POINTS

- Scores of startups fail based not on the business concept, but on the implementation. Countless great ideas have been destroyed by less-than-great processes.
- A *Harvard Business Review* study concluded that only 8 percent of all business leaders are good at both strategy and execution. Process is usually the part that earns short shrift. It isn't sexy. It doesn't earn as many headlines as a new concept. Business leaders tend to focus more on ideas than process.
- To correct this and enhance your businesses chances for success, start first with a change in mindset. Make process an equal partner to innovation. Spread that commitment to staff and create a culture that values and rewards process. Make sure budgeting and staff allocation reflect the emphasis.
- Take steps to ensure your process is adaptable and sustainable. Test it out with best-case and worst-case scenarios. Then adapt benchmarks and measurables to guarantee it remains a top priority.

Visit Collaboration-LLC.com for a whitepaper titled, "When You're the Bottleneck," and a webinar titled, "When You Are the Bottleneck to Business Growth."

E-MYTH BUSTING

> **E-Myth: Being an entrepreneur means being your own boss.**
> **E-Reality: Being an entrepreneur means more servitude than ever.**

If you work at a company, you probably have only one or two bosses. When you start a company, everyone is your boss. Your board and advisors set your goals. Your clients devour your thoughts and energy. Your staff makes demands on your time. It feels like everyone is pulling on you, especially during the early months and years.

Worse, thanks to cell phones and portable computers, you're always on the job. It's your company. You can't not think about it. Company worries start to creep into your dreams. Vacations? Forget about them. Even if you could take some time off, your brain wouldn't let you.

If it's freedom you crave, better to take a job as a Bedouin.

CHAPTER 11

CRASH AND BURNOUT

I have a friend. I know him well. Too well. He was the stereotypical entrepreneur. He launched a string of businesses as a boy, mowing lawns and delivering newspapers. He loved the feel of money in his pocket (even though he became an ATM for his many brothers and sisters). He landed his first job at 15, making milkshakes at McDonalds®. After a few months on the job, he received a promotion to French fry cook. He fantasized about being the next Ray Kroc.

After college, he worked for several large corporations throughout the South, gathering valuable, firsthand knowledge about how businesses succeeded and failed. He rose through the ranks quickly, accumulating larger salaries and loftier titles.

But the desire to run his own company burned too bright. It's what he'd craved since childhood. He looked at the business pages and saw entrepreneur after entrepreneur striking it rich. Jeff Bezos. Larry Page. Martha Stewart. Mark Zuckerberg. His heroes.

So, he decided to gather his life savings and start a small consulting firm. He had the skills, the background, and most importantly, the desire to make the firm a success. He rented some office space and started to hustle.

And he experienced success right away. Fellow business owners liked this guy and his services. They hired him and told others to do the same. My friend needed to assemble a staff, and quick. He built a team and told them, "Follow my lead."

After a few years of this, the business began to plateau. The firm treaded water, gaining a client here, losing another there. He couldn't understand why his business wasn't growing. That frustration began to take a toll.

My friend beat himself up daily. He couldn't sleep because of all the worries. So he vowed to work longer hours and eschew vacation days. He rode his staff to do the same. He became short tempered when employees fell short of his expectations. He sent emails at 3 a.m. and called staff on the weekends. Several left his firm for other jobs, sending him into a panic.

He began to drink more and gain weight. His relationship suffered as his business sputtered. Suddenly everything in his life felt like a downward spiral. The more his business stalled, the less he slept, the more irritable he became, and the worse he acted as a person both inside the office and out.

He told me he felt like an imposter, even though he was seen by everyone as a successful businessman and model citizen. In his mind he was a big phony. "If people only knew the truth," he told me.

I tried to remind him of his lifetime of accomplishments and his many unique skills, but he didn't listen. I then tried to tell him about "imposter syndrome"[132] and how it's a real and common occurrence that afflicts successful people at all levels, making them believe they aren't worthy. I suggested a mental health counselor. He wouldn't have it.

"I feel like I'm going to have a heart attack," he told himself with increasing regularity. "All of these other entrepreneurs have been able to pull it off, why can't I? There must be something wrong with me. Deeply wrong."

He thought technology would solve all his problems, so he shifted the focus of his business from consulting to software. But the issues wouldn't go away. In fact, they got worse.

He wanted to give up, to turn in his resignation. He thought back to the entrepreneurial spirit he possessed as a boy and young man, all the dreams of success, riches, and freedom. Instead, he had debt, doubt, and depression. He seemed ready to snap.

My friends, that friend is me.

I'm like almost every entrepreneur I've ever met.

The entrepreneurial hype machine focuses on the spoils and ignores the realities of starting and growing a business. Sure, the machine talks about hard work, but rarely do you hear about the toll a new business takes on physical and mental health, on families and marriage, on every aspect of your life and the lives of those around you.

The solution most often prescribed? Work harder! The entrepreneurial culture celebrates things we know to be

---

[132] https://www.nytimes.com/2018/06/12/smarter-living/dealing-with-impostor-syndrome-when-youre-treated-as-an-impostor.html

harmful. Sometimes lethal. How many times have you heard entrepreneurs brag about the hours they work or the million things they're doing at once?

I had a boss who loved to tell us he hadn't had a day off in 10 years. *Wow!* I marveled at the time. *That's what it takes to be successful.* That's the culture to which I aspired. I also had a workaholic colleague who had a heart attack in her 40s. I knew the stresses of her job played a major role in her health, yet still I clocked 12-hour days and refused to take a holiday.

I was far from alone. Americans lead the world in unused vacation days. According to the travel industry (and they monitor these things closely), more than half of all Americans didn't use all their vacation time last year, a total of more than 700 million days![133] This despite the fact that we only allot a few weeks a year of vacation time to begin with. We don't give employees six-week summer holidays or two-week ski breaks like they do in Europe. Yet we still don't use up all our time!

Sad, because we know the extra hours at work don't always lead to more productivity. Studies have found the opposite to be true. Researchers argue working more than 40–50 hours a week results in rapidly diminishing returns.[134] It also leads to increased costs for the businesses—everything from overtime hours, to more expensive utility bills, to additional man hours to correct all the shoddy work made by someone burning the midnight oil.

---

[133] https://projecttimeoff.com/reports/state-of-american-vacation-2018/

[134] https://hbr.org/2015/08/the-research-is-clear-long-hours-backfire-for-people-and-for-companies

Henry Ford realized this a century ago. He saw a big spike in problems as soon as his employees worked more than 40 hours a week. The industrialist limited workers to 40 hours and watched his production soar.[135]

Many of the world's top economies understand the disastrous impacts of overworking as well. Great Britain, Germany, France, Sweden, Finland, and Denmark all place limits on the workweek.[136] They know it hurts everyone involved—the business, the employees, the government, and the public at large. Finnish researchers found that overworking leads to elevated levels of stress, heavy drinking, sleep loss, diabetes, memory impairment, and heart disease.[137]

U.S. researchers have concluded the same,[138] yet we still glorify the workaholic. I certainly did. I experienced nearly all those harmful side effects and convinced myself I could work through them all. If I could just land that new client, if I could just grow my software sales, everything would be fine; I'd be back on the path to becoming the next Richard Branson or Oprah Winfrey.

It wasn't until I hit rock bottom and fled for my sabbatical that I realized no number of hours would solve my problems. I didn't need to work harder. I needed to work smarter.

This is a common occurrence. Most entrepreneurs and business leaders are stubborn mofos. I was. It takes something

---

[135] http://www.asianefficiency.com/mindsets/diminishing-returns-working-more-does-not-mean-getting-more-done/

[136] https://www.inc.com/geoffrey-james/stop-working-more-than-40-hours-a-week.html

[137] https://hbr.org/2015/08/the-research-is-clear-long-hours-backfire-for-people-and-for-companies

[138] https://projecttimeoff.com/blog/doctors-orders-take-a-vacation/

dramatic for us to change our views—a bankruptcy, a divorce, the loss of a big client, or the departure of a key associate. Then, and only then, do we reconsider our choices. Sometimes we never do.

But it doesn't have to be this way. I wish I could've broken out of my pigheadedness years ago and seen that my common errors of acting like a selfish entrepreneur were not only killing my business, but they were also killing me.

Burnout is the dirty little secret of the business world, especially when you're starting your own. Very few business leaders have had the courage to talk about it, fearful it may hurt their career or their company. I get it. I cringed at the thought of anyone knowing my secret. I imagined my clients would terminate their agreements with me once they found out I was struggling.

What I didn't know was that almost all of them were struggling too. For some, it was hitting a wall or falling out of love with a business idea they'd brought to life. They'd grown bored. Or frustrated. They felt like they'd been sold a bill of goods about running a business, but the reality was far from the starry notion depicted in the media. The myth of entrepreneurship highlights all the joys and rewards while downplaying the agony and sacrifice and exhaustive hours.

Others were, like me, on the verge of shuttering their operations or turning over the reins to someone else. They were at the breaking point. They could see their companies beginning to fray, and their employees could see it as well. Still, they remained silent. To this day, rare is the business leader who will be open about it.

Lloyds Banking Group's Chief António Horta-Osório is one of the few who has talked about mental health in the workplace. In 2011, the company announced Horta-Osório would take a two-month leave due to "extreme fatigue." He had grown so exhausted from the stresses and round-the-clock nature of his job, his doctors demanded he take an extended break.

The announcement caused the bank's shares to slump, a trend that continued over the next few weeks amid uncertainty over Lloyds' management team.

Companies like Lloyds are inexperienced and ill-equipped to handle situations like executive burnout. The bank appointed an interim chief, Tim Tookey, and even announced a second backup plan in case Mr. Horta-Osório's leave of absence extended into the following year.

But the time away did Horta-Osório good. He returned to work in January 2012 and remains CEO, enlisting other senior managers to help shoulder his workload. He's also made it a priority to bring workplace mental health issues into the open in the hope his employees and those at other businesses will seek treatment when needed.

"When an employee breaks a leg or suffers an infection, we know how to respond," he wrote.[139] "Mental health should be dealt with in the same way. With a culture of adequate support and sufficient time off, an employee can return to work with confidence and without embarrassment."

Under Horta-Osório's leadership, Lloyds partnered with Mental Health UK to highlight the link between financial

---

[139] https://www.theguardian.com/commentisfree/2018/may/01/removeing-taboo-mental-health-work-lloyds-banking-group-antonio-horta-osorio

problems and mental health.[140] The team offered expanded services to employees and convinced a growing number of workers to seek company-provided professional help.

Horta-Osório also knew burnout and depression hit senior business leaders like himself. He wanted to do something about it:

> "I personally have been involved in a ground-breaking programme which we called 'optimal leadership resilience.' This is designed to help senior leaders at Lloyds to think about and put in place actions that help them build personal resilience and positive wellbeing. The programme covers nutrition, heart monitoring, sleep management, mindfulness, psychological testing and analysis. After the group executive committee and our top 200 senior leaders, the programme is now being extended to the next 2,000 group leaders, which means they can support their own teams when they see signs that someone may be struggling."[141]

The programs are progressive and innovative. But the most meaningful thing Horta-Osório has done for his company is come forward and talk about his own struggles. His openness will reverberate for a long time.

There's a conventional wisdom in business that in order to be successful you need to marry your job. You need to

---

[140] https://www.mentalhealth-uk.org/latest-news/lloyds-banking-group-joins-forces-with-mental-health-uk/

[141] https://www.theguardian.com/commentisfree/2018/may/01/removeing-taboo-mental-health-work-lloyds-banking-group-antonio-horta-osorio

think about it 24/7; you need to let it consume you. Nothing could be farther from the truth.

In my experience, managers who let their business consume their every waking hour are awful leaders. They're typically impatient, demanding, unhealthy, closed to outside ideas, and not very interesting or inspiring.

I checked every one of these boxes myself. In the early years of my business, I had a partner. Poor soul. I demanded the world out of both of us. I'd phone her in the middle of the night with an idea that could've waited until morning. I'd give her grief for family time or even sick days. I pushed, and pushed, and pushed...until she quit, taking a job with a client who paid her far more and gave her much less grief.

I wasn't an evil person. I loved this partner and wanted her to succeed. I wanted us to succeed together. I just behaved like I thought entrepreneurs needed to behave. Mush, mush, mush! Instead, my business and our relationship turned to mush.

It wasn't until after my sabbatical that I realized less is more. If you're burning yourself out, you're probably burning your team out as well. My partner told me she felt like she was in "an abusive relationship." The words stung...but rang true. An all-consuming, 24/7, relentless entrepreneur is often an abusive leader. Abusive to himself and his family, abusive to his staff, abusive to everyone he encounters.

Finding balance is that final, key step in the evolution from entrepreneurial leader to successful collaborative leader. I'm talking about balance in family time and work life; office hours and restorative hours; physical health and mental health; the amount of sleep you're getting each night, and the alcohol you're consuming; the ability to focus at work and then turn it off at home.

Don't get me wrong. I know as well as anyone the amount of hard work, long hours, and stress that goes into creating a business. Normal levels are manageable. Anything more is lethal. If you're feeling burned out, I can guarantee you your staff is too. And I'm guessing your company profits are starting to unravel as well.

So give yourself a break, both mentally and physically. Take some time to take stock of your life. If you're not healthy and feeling energized, no one at your company will be. Head off on an extended vacation. Or just go to a beach for a long weekend and ask yourself a series of important questions: How's my mental health? When do I feel most stressed? How's my work-life balance? Do I turn off work when I come home, or do I check emails at all hours? Do I need a glass of wine (or two or three) at the end of every day?

Next, I encourage leaders to look to others for inspiration. Do they know someone who appears to live a balanced and successful life? Talk to those people. Learn about their approach. What rules or limits did they institute to help ensure a healthy work life?

Need more inspiration? Look to Cheryl Sandberg, the COO of Facebook. She has one of the most demanding jobs on the planet, and yet she leaves the office at a reasonable hour. "I walk out of this office every day at 5:30 so I'm home for dinner with my kids at 6:00, and interestingly, I've been doing that since I had kids," she said in a video for Makers. com.[142] "I did that when I was at Google, I did that here, and I would say it's not until the last year, two years, that I'm brave

---

[142] https://www.inc.com/jessica-stillman/facebook-sheryl-sandberg-can-leave-early-why-arent-you.html

enough to talk about it publicly. Now I certainly wouldn't lie, but I wasn't running around giving speeches on it."

Sandberg is wise to set hard and fast limits on her time. If she didn't, the demands of the office could consume her. She's also spot-on about a budding change in the culture where business leaders can now open up about work-life balance.

And remember Richard Branson, founder of Virgin Megastores? In addition to taking every August off to holiday with his family, Branson gives his employees "unlimited vacation time." He allows his salaried staff to choose when and how long they vacation. "We are human beings not human doings—so let's start acting like it, by taking the time simply to be and appreciate the beauty of the world," he wrote on his company blog.[143] "Remember to be as well as to do, and if that proves hard, add it as a bullet point to your next to-do list, or put it in your work calendar as you would a meeting." Bravo.

Netflix has had a similar unlimited vacation policy since 2004.[144] It doesn't seem to have slowed the company down one iota. Employees are still required to accomplish their responsibilities and perform at a high level. But company management empowers them to make these decisions on their own and through collaborative discussions with colleagues.

A growing number of collaborative business leaders are realizing the dangers of overworking and are taking creative steps to combat the stress. eBay CEO John Donahue likes to take "thinking days" away from the office.[145] Ford Motor

---

[143] https://www.virgin.com/richard-branson/get-out-office

[144] https://www.entrepreneur.com/article/269989

[145] https //www.lifehack.org/articles/work/these-highly-successful-people-tell-you-take-vacations-from-work.html

Company Chairman Bill Ford meditates every day without fail. LinkedIn CEO Jeff Weiner recommends a meditation app to employees and others.[146]

Ryan Holmes is the founder and CEO of Hootsuite®, and a collaborative leader who turned part of the company's headquarters into a makeshift gym. "We're a technology company with around 1,000 employees, not a gym. But from the start, I've built fitness into how we do business. For health, for morale and, yes, for the bottom line, it's the best decision we could have made."[147]

Mark Bertolini, the CEO of Aetna, embraced yoga as a way to help him recover from an accident. After experiencing the numerous benefits firsthand, he introduced yoga into the company culture. More than 12,500 employees have participated in company sponsored sessions.[148]

Promega™ is a Madison, Wisconsin-based biotech company with a portfolio of more than 4,000 products and roughly 1,500 employees around the world. Promega Biosciences, the branch located here in San Luis Obispo, has long upheld the organization's efforts to encourage employees' personal and professional development. For years, Promega Biosciences has offered initiatives to support healthy lifestyle choices, which include providing free community bicycles, giving financial rewards for participation in physical activities

---

[146] https://www.businessinsider.com/5-successful-leaders-that-have-used-meditation-to-be-more-productive-2018-4

[147] https://www.inc.com/linkedin/ryan-holmes/why-its-time-we-paid-employees-exercise-work-ryan-holmes.html

[148] https://www.nytimes.com/2018/09/21/business/mark-bertolini-aetna-corner-office.html.

outside the office, and offering programs that support breaking harmful habits like smoking.

Over the last several years, these programs have been strengthened by adding support around emotional well-being. The company's ESI (emotional and social intelligence) program has been a multi-layered approach toward bolstering employee engagement and satisfaction both in the workplace and at home. Global initiatives include mindfulness training, regular group meditation, and "mindful leadership" courses. Promega Biosciences was the first branch to implement an ESI catalyst team. This peer-to-peer group is tasked with spreading the tenets of ESI, including "say what needs to be said with courage and compassion" and "encourage diverse perspectives." The success of this group has led to the formation of several catalyst teams at company headquarters in Madison.

The importance and support placed on these initiatives from all levels of management have allowed Promega to create a holistic view of employee well-being. What's blossomed from it not only increased employee satisfaction but boosted positivity and the sense of ownership in each person's role toward the company's progress.

Stress release can also come without lifting a finger. I have a friend who has a "95 Percent Rule" at work. He's a perfectionist who had the tendency to pick a project to death. He used to have an impossible time letting things go, especially his writings. He'd spend hours agonizing over sentence structure or the perfect word to use. He knew he was spending far too much time on many tasks. So he created this 95 Percent Rule to counter his tendency toward perfectionism. Whenever he thought a project was 95 percent complete, he'd let it go. Sound advice.

Other successful business leaders I counsel make it a point to unplug—literally and figuratively. They advise staff not to contact them after work hours unless there's an emergency. And jammed printers or internet inquiries aren't emergencies. They turn off their cellphones and refuse to check email at home. In turn, they vow not to send emails, text messages, or voicemails to staff unless absolutely essential.

Businesses have insatiable appetites. They'll devour every ounce of time and energy you offer them. So set hard limits, actively communicate them, and don't give in.

For me, breakfast meetings are out of the question, and weekends are sacrosanct. I've told myself and my staff that I will take at least two extended vacations overseas each year and carve out several long weekends when possible. I've stuck to that plan for the past eight years. And guess what? My business didn't crater in my absence! In fact, it thrived.

My staff did too. They broadened their capabilities and enjoyed running the operation on their own. Now they goad me to take more time off. "You sure you don't want to go on another vacation, Michael? Italy is nice this time of year. Or maybe Thailand? A long train ride across Canada?"

Another key for me and other business leaders is to make office hours more productive. That means limiting distractions such as Facebook, other social media, or nonwork emails. Gather your staff and talk with them about this. Lead by example and watch productivity soar. Let them know that you want them to enjoy their vacations, weekends, and free time… and to do so means giving work full focus during office hours.

The biggest change I've made in my management style since my sabbatical is to delegate, delegate, delegate. And damn, it feels so good! Entrepreneurs tend to hold on to every responsibility, believing if they don't do it nobody will. And in many cases, that's true.

But collaborative business leaders need to do the exact opposite. Loosen up. Let it go. Delegate. Start with something small such as office supplies or mailing operations. Be clear with your colleagues about exactly what you expect and your preferences for how the tasks should be completed. Then turn them loose.

If you're like me, you'll realize you've been holding on to these tasks for far too long, exhale deeply, and look for more jobs to delegate. Entrepreneurs are addicted to control. Collaborative business leaders are addicted to delegation.

For my clients who struggle with delegating, I pull out a legal notepad and start going through the numbers. I show them that their time is money, so time spent on lesser tasks is money and opportunity tossed out the window. I role-play scenarios with them. Let's say the company doubles in size, or triples. Are you still going to be answering phones? At some point you must loosen your grip. So why not now? Start slowly, then vow to delegate more each time your company reaches a certain benchmark. Deal?

My friends and fellow professionals joke that I talk too much about my sabbatical. They say I'm like that college kid who spent a summer in Europe, lived in the hostels with the backpackers, then came back to the United States blabbering about baguettes and gondola rides.

They're right. I do talk about it at every opportunity I get. But not because of the trip itself. No, for me the lasting benefit of the trip wasn't a series of museum visits or leisurely lunches. My sabbatical was a demarcation point. It was the big eye-opener, the "aha" moment when I realized I needed to stop acting like an entrepreneur and mature into a collaborative businessman.

Frankly, I wish the realization happened years earlier. I wish I didn't need to go halfway around the world to see it. Some of us are slow learners. Or stubborn. Or both.

When I talk about my sabbatical, my goal is to inspire your inspiration. Bon voyage.

SUMMARY POINTS

- "Me" business leaders put a lot on their shoulders. They frequently allow their businesses to consume their lives and consequently have higher than average rates of divorce, depression, sleep depravity, stress, and addiction.
- Burnout is a common yet underreported phenomenon in the business world. I would know. I'm a burnout victim myself.
- To save yourself (and your business), take stock in your mental health, seek professional help if necessary, and begin crafting a new work-life balance.
- Gain inspiration from fellow business leaders. Learn how they set parameters on their time, expand vacation policies, meditate, make gym visits part of every day, do yoga or take regular walks, unplug from their devices, or take a sabbatical.
  See how they work fewer hours but more productive hours, how they delegate, and learn not to sweat the small stuff.
- Installing a healthy work-life balance is the final step in the shift from struggling "me" business leader to successful "we" business leader.

CHAPTER 12

MAKING THE SHIFT

In the past, pride and ego prevented me from letting go and shifting my mindset. Hubris remains one of the most lethal and widespread forces in business. Ego is also a chronic condition, something you can never get rid of but can only attempt to control. In fact, you'd be foolish to try to eliminate pride and ego. It exists even in the humblest among us.

The wiser course is to acknowledge ego, allow it to have a say, but never let it take over the meeting. Pass the microphone over to ego's opposite. Altruism. Modesty. Unselfishness. What do they have to say? Know that ego is a part of you, but not solely you. You're still in charge of your life and your business. Put it into its proper place and move forward.

In business, and in life, ego is overrated. I'm reminded of the story of the young man who started his adult life consumed with what people thought of him. By the time he reached 40, he was set in his ways and paid less attention to what people thought. But it wasn't until he turned 60 that he realized people were never thinking of him in the first place. They were too consumed with their lives, their egos.

This could have been me. But once I realized that I was running my business like an entrepreneur with ADD, I began taking the steps to forge trust and empower my employees. I learned to disclose more, to be open about good news and bad, to stop trying to solve everyone's challenges. I learned it was fine, preferred even, to let them try and fail. They would grow, and so would the company. I learned to let go, and they learned to grab hold. Together, we adopted the tools, training, and processes needed for them to succeed. Then we constantly checked in with each other to see if and when the system needed tweaks.

Much of my change in attitude stemmed from improved communication. This started with me. I admitted to myself and others that I hadn't been the best communicator. I talked enough, but I didn't listen enough. I saw company communication as top-down rather than a communal give-and-take.

I've learned to counter this by bringing in my employees earlier in the decision-making process, spending more time talking about "why" we are doing something, and soliciting input at every stage. I also know I'm human and bound to slip up at any time. So I've tried to do a series of daily self-checks: What's my tone and my body language like when I talk with my employees? Am I keeping my promises? Is there anything else they need to know to help them do their jobs?

My changes in communication have led to their changes in communication. My younger employees, like all younger generations, communicate differently. They're more comfortable communicating through technology. Technology isn't going away; it's infiltrating more and more corners of our business operations.

So instead of fighting it or insisting my staff and I communicate through the methods I prefer, we've learned to strike a balance. So far, so good. They've also helped me, and the company as a whole, tell our story with our hearts as well as our heads. I've realized that nobody roots for a brand or a company. Instead, they cheer for the stories behind the products or the personal tales behind the company.

Like many other business executives, the old entrepreneur in me insisted on sticking to traditional marketing and messaging, proclaiming that everything is great, the sky's the limit, and we're going to change the world! The collaborative leader in me wanted to find those areas of commonality where we connect as humans. It's about cutting out the BS and getting real, both inside the company and out.

My team allowed this to happen for me. I thought back to my return from Europe on the first sabbatical, telling them I had a revelation, that our struggling company had failed to make the shift from entrepreneurial startup to mature, collaborative operation. We needed wholesale change, I preached, not just a few adjustments. I wanted to make these changes with them.

Some embraced the new direction, some hesitated, some left. But we entered the new era together, vowing to put our egos aside and make smart decisions, ones that would be constantly evaluated and challenged to see if there was ever a better course.

The toughest change was the one I saw hampering most of the companies we counseled: accountability. I showed them the Harvard study that concluded, "One out of every two managers is terrible at accountability" and admitted I was part of the "One." I attributed this to a desire to be liked and to my tendency to act like an entrepreneur who has long been accountable to no one. I knew I needed to make a shift from a "do as I say" boss to a "what do you need to do your job" coach.

On the flip side, my staff helped me understand that they preferred greater accountability, feeling that they needed to be held accountable at every step to do their jobs better. This didn't mean more browbeating or micromanaging, it just meant being clear with each other about the expectations of the job. We instituted ways to better define expectations, offer feedback, set realistic timelines, and fine-tune the process as we went along.

I'm still guilty of being conflict averse from time to time, and I never relish a tough conversation. But now I realize that when I fail to properly address an issue, my business suffers. I constantly ask myself, "Is my tendency to be a people pleaser helping or hurting us?"

And I trust in the process we've established over the last five years. I remember being a young and hungry entrepreneur, cringing at the word "process." I was an innovator, not a manager! I gave process short shrift and our business suffered. I saw the same thing happening in businesses all around us.

There are millions of million-dollar ideas, and thousands of companies that start off with rich promise. The ones that flourish and continue to grow are the ones that embrace the details, companies that are just as fanatical about execution as they are about ideas. It's a matter of getting the balance right.

Once I shifted my mindset and achieved this balance for myself and my business, I headed over to Europe for a second time. The last story I read before I left made me chuckle. Elon Musk, taking time out from running Tesla, and SpaceX, and SolarCity, and the Boring Company, had attempted to help rescue a group of Thai boys trapped in an underwater cave. He offered to build a small submarine that would pull the boys out one-by-one. He posted videos of a prototype on social media and even flew to the cave in Thailand with the sub.[149]

The rescue team declined his offer, instead organizing a successful effort that involved outfitting the boys with scuba masks, then navigating them through the cave on stretchers. The world breathed a sigh of relief.

In the aftermath, when asked about Musk's plan, Thai officials and cavers involved with the rescue dismissed the offer as nothing more than a "PR stunt."[150] They pointed out that Musk's submarine would never be able to navigate the tight passages and hard turns to reach the boys. Musk fired back, calling one British diver involved with the rescue a "pedo guy," insinuating he was a pedophile. Musk later apologized.

A week later he jumped into another high-profile crisis, vowing to help clean the drinking water in Flint, Michigan. "Please consider this a commitment that I will fund fixing the water in any house in Flint that has water contamination above FDA levels. No kidding," he tweeted. Musk held true

[149] https://www.vox.com/2018/7/18/17576302/elon-musk-thai-cave-rescue-submarine

[150] https://www.vox.com/2018/7/18/17576302/elon-musk-thai-cave-rescue-submarine

to his word, donating more than $480,000,[151] which allowed schools to install drinking fountains with ultraviolet filtration systems.[152] He promised to do more in the future as the city works to replace miles of lead pipes.

I salute Musk for his commitment to helping others. I don't question his motives or belittle any offer of assistance. But if I was one of his shareholders, I would be much happier with the way he helped in Flint, by writing a check, than by the way he inserted himself into the Thailand cave rescue, flying over with a device that no one seemed to want.

There's a business lesson there, I told myself. Musk is the embodiment of "chasing sexy" at his companies, jumping from one headline-grabbing initiative to another instead of bearing down and focusing on the core elements. That restlessness seemed to carry over into his charitable efforts.

But maybe he learned something from the public reactions to his Thailand assistance versus the help he provided to Flint. And maybe that realization will carry over into his business practices as well. If Elon Musk can pull back on "chasing sexy," we all can.

For me, this started with doing the research about entrepreneurship and successful businesses. I stressed myself time and again thinking I was the only fool on the planet not smart enough to grow a thriving, mature business. I thought overnight internet millionaires and unicorn businesses were commonplace; or that businesses would be successful if the

---

[151] http://fortune.com/2018/10/08/musk-gives-clean-water-flint-schools/

[152] https://www.cnn.com/2018/10/08/us/elon-musk-flint-schools-water-filtration-trnd/index.html

entrepreneur worked hard enough, came up with brilliant ideas, and gave a great speech.

The more I looked at business magazines and online profiles of successful entrepreneurs, the worse I felt about myself and my struggling business—like people who read a fashion magazine and feel they're fat and ugly compared to the beautiful people in the advertisements and photo shoots.

Well, the pictures in *Vogue* or *Elle* or *GQ* aren't real. The models have been heavily made-up and staged, and the photos have been doctored to remove every little blemish and imperfection. The business magazines do exactly the same!

So I put down the magazines and dug deeper into the facts. I uncovered a business landscape that bared scant semblance to the tall tales and public perceptions of entrepreneurship. Now when I see and meet entrepreneurs, I know their businesses need a lot of hard work and smart thinking. I also know they need a lot of luck, help from others, and a much clearer picture of the challenges they face.

They need a change in mindset. Just like I desperately did. They need to see that the single most important step they can take is evolving from an entrepreneurial mindset to a collaborative one—a shift from "me" to "we."

CONCLUSION

THE ROAD AHEAD

The pilgrim trail Via Francigena translates to "the road from France," but it actually stretches all the way to England. The ancient foot trail runs for nearly 1,300 miles and dates back to AD 990, when an archbishop of Canterbury named Sigeric walked to Rome in order to receive honors from Pope John XV. The detailed notes of his chosen paths led to the creation of one of the most popular pilgrimage routes of the Middle Ages.[153]

The Via Francigena has undergone a rebirth of late. The Council of Europe named it a historic Cultural Route, and the governments of England, Switzerland, France, and Italy have since invested significant funds to improve the trail and encourage visitors. It still receives just a fraction of the

---

[153] https://www.nytimes.com/2016/09/11/travel/via-francigena-tuscany.html

tourists who opt for the better-known Camino de Santiago in Spain.

And that was just fine for Steve and me as we headed out from our Italian villa to inspect the Via Francigena for ourselves. I can't say we were religious pilgrims or in search of anything other than a peaceful walk and a glass of wine. Still, I could see why Sigeric took the time to record the details of the trail, here and now winding its way over green hills dappled with olive groves and vineyards. In the distance, the 14 medieval stone towers of San Gimignano waved to us like a set of hands. There used to be more than 70. No wonder locals refer to the town as the "Manhattan of the Middle Ages."

On a whim, Steve and I decided to join several members of my family for the trip to Tuscany, staying at a 300-year-old farmhouse outside San Gimignano and taking day trips to soul-restoring towns such as Volterra and Siena. We filled our days in the farmers markets, looking for the perfect fennel sausage or fresh bell pepper. Each meal featured copious amounts of wine, cheese, pastries, and breads. We laughed with my siblings about the insanity of growing up in a family with 17 kids.

On past trips, I took at least a week to slow down into "vacation mode." On this one, it took about 20 minutes. Steve, too. On our first day in Italy, I raised a midday glass of the area's renowned Vernaccia white wine and toasted him. Toasted us. It had been five years to the day since the sabbatical that changed my business. And my life.

Though the technology made it much easier to connect back home, on this trip there were no checked emails, no calls to the office, no documents to review. I chuckled to myself thinking about my sneaky ways during the sabbatical, how I ducked into the internet cafes while Steve slept in, always remembering to bring him coffees and pastries to complete the ruse. The thought of wasting a morning in some dingy internet cafe made me cringe now. I'll go with the afternoon card games and town square meanders, thank you.

And leisurely walks on the Via Francigena. On this day, Steve and I told ourselves we'd walk until we tired. Or stumbled upon the perfect place to idle away an afternoon.

We found it at a hillside pensione a few kilometers off the trail—Torraccia di Chiusi, with its rolling vineyards and alluring stone patio beneath a grove of pine trees. Within minutes, Maria, the proprietor, plopped down a tray of their wines and cheeses and boasted about Chef Bruno's pasta. Sold. We had the entire patio to ourselves.

Brilliant man that Sigeric. The sensual pleasures and warm hospitality he documented a thousand years prior remained in abundance to this day. Steve and I talked about our five- to seven-year dream to phase out of our current jobs and move to Barcelona, spending the remainder of our free time visiting places just like this.

Our journey was not as epic as Sigeric's, and we still had work to make our dreams a reality, but damn, we had come a long way over the past half-decade.

I remembered ruining the mood of many a meal during our initial sabbatical, fretting about petty office issues or botched client relations. I still had the tendency to worry. I think all business leaders have a healthy amount of anxiety in them. But there's a big difference in me today. The anxiety doesn't consume me, it pushes me to perform better. When I feel that old internal voice popping up, wanting me to stress about a work matter, a louder, more confident voice usually calms the situation and puts things into perspective.

After all, we had a new, more senior team in place now. In the past, I would've felt threatened by high-level executives on staff. Now, here on the winery patio, as the afternoon sun dulled, I raised a glass to them. Cheers. Thanks for letting me slip away.

Maria plopped down a big ol' plate of homemade pasta with a garden tomato sauce. How do Italians make such simple ingredients so delectable? Chef Bruno doesn't "chase sexy!" His menu isn't weighed down with dozens of offerings and endless ingredients. He cooks a handful of dishes using fresh, local ingredients, and he cooks them well.

As Steve plowed into the pasta, I mentally drifted for a split second back to my office. And only for a split second. I thought we should have a company retreat at a place like Torraccia di Chiusi or maybe on the grounds of one of our winery clients in Paso Robles. I made a mental list of vintners to call.

I didn't worry about office operations. I knew things would run well in my absence. Better, we all joked. I didn't tell them that I was only half-joking. I knew my time away would allow them to grow and flourish in their jobs. I had complete confidence they would do so.

I felt light years away from the first sabbatical, when I hadn't trained them properly, hadn't empowered them to do their jobs, and hadn't established those crucial bonds of mutual trust. Part of me back then expected to return to a closed office. Part of me would've been relieved.

Reclining in our seats, Steve and I chatted about the side trips we wanted to take while living in Barcelona—summer weeks on the Costa del Sol or getaways to the French Riviera. It all seemed so much closer now, a doable to-do list rather than a pie-in-the-sky fantasy. I felt like I had taken control of my business rather than letting it control me. We didn't talk about business. Or the news.

Steve and I contemplated ordering some more wine. I demurred. Another bottle and I think we would've had to spend the night rather than walk back to the villa. But the real reason I abstained was because I wanted to soak in everything surrounding me at that moment—the crunch of the gravel driveway, faint wafts from the potted roses, Maria's laugh from the kitchen. Right here, right now, is exactly where I want to be.

As Steve paid the bill, I went over to Maria to give her a hug and thank her for a lovely afternoon, an enjoyable and restorative couple of hours. We'd return, I promised. Hopefully sooner rather than later. Steve told her "grazia" as well, and we began our walk back home.

Maybe it was the wine, or the sensory abundance, or just the unadulterated happiness of the moment. But I felt warm, and strong, and ready to amble until sunset and well into the night. I wanted the moment, the day, to last. I felt healthy, both physically and mentally—the exact opposite of how I felt the last go-around.

Of all the changes I had made at my own business and instituted at hundreds of other companies over the last five years, the most crucial was getting my mind right. I no longer wanted to give up, give in, or give my notice to someone. I wanted to see my company grow into a legacy business, able to thrive long after I had left the picture. The burnout I had experienced felt like it had happened in another life. Now the burn came from within, a desire to continue to help my business mature and thrive.

Steve and I ambled along at a leisurely pace. I knew I was far from home, and there were sure to be a few bumps in the road. But I knew I was now on a much better path, and I looked forward to the journey ahead.

RESOURCES

Visit http://www.Collaboration-llc.com for the Collaboration Business Consulting Resource Center for Business Leaders to access and review the below content.

WHITEPAPERS

- Three Pitfalls of an Entrepreneur That Kill Your Business (Chapter 2)
- Online Quiz (Chapter 3)
- Core Elements of Strategic Planning (Chapter 4)
- Strategic Plan vs. Implementation Plan: Know the Difference (Chapter 4)
- Leadership vs. Management: Why a Growing Business Needs Both (Chapter 5)
- Best Practices to Successfully Lead Your Management Team (Chapter 6)
- The Management Dilemma (Chapter 7)
- How to Empower Your Team to Succeed Using the Freedom Scale (Chapter 8)

263

- Maintaining Sustainable Profitability (Chapter 9)
- When You're the Bottleneck (Chapter 10)

WEBINARS

- Webinar: Why Being an Entrepreneur is Killing Your Business (Chapter 2)
- Webinar: Strategic Plan vs. Implementation Plan (Chapter 4)
- Webinar: The Management Dilemma (Chapter 7)
- Webinar: When You Are the Bottleneck to Business Growth (Chapter 10)

CASE STUDIES

- Adjusting the Viewpoint: How a Leading San Francisco Signage Company Unlocked Their Future Potential
- Creating a Scalable Business: Pushing Past a Plateau in an E-commerce and Manufacturing Company
- Engaging in Sustainable Growth: How Construction Companies Can Thrive
- Creating a Powerful Culture: Shaping a Family-Owned Insurance Agency for Future Success
- Bridging the Gap: Techniques for Leaping to the Next Level of Business Growth

INTERVIEWS

- Wine with an Entrepreneur: Rob Kitzman with Kitzman Culligan Water

- Wine with an Entrepreneur: Juliana Sommer with Priority Architectural Graphics
- Wine with an Entrepreneur: Rick Stollmeyer with MINDBODY
- Wine with an Entrepreneur: Joni Anderson with Anderson Burton Construction
- Wine with an Entrepreneur: Shannon Larrabee with Central Coast Distributing

BIBLIOGRAPHY

Andersen, E. (2013, October 7). It seemed like a good idea at the time: 7 of the worst business decisions ever made. *Forbes*. https://www.forbes.com/sites/erikaandersen/2013/10/04/it-seemed-like-a-good-idea-at-the-time-7-of-the-worst-business-decisions-ever-made/ (footnote 19)

Apparel Resources. (2018, January 8). *Forever 21 closing down non-performing stores*. Apparel Resources. https://apparelresources.com/business-news/retail/forever-21-closing-non-performing-stores/. (footnote 62)

Becher, J. (2015, August 12). 6 quotes to help you understand why it's important to say no. *Forbes*. https://www.forbes.com/sites/sap/2015/08/12/quotes-on-saying-no/#222e33625555. (footnote 48)

Berthiaume, D. (2019, July 28). *Report: Forever 21 Seeks smaller stores, loan*. Chain Store Age. https://www.chainstoreage.com/real-estate/report-forever-1-seeks-smaller-stores-loan/. (footnote 64)

Biography.com Editors. (2020, June 22). *George Eastman*. Biography.com. https://www.biography.com/people/george-eastman-9283428. (footnote 75)

Biography.com Editors. (2021, April 7). *Elon Musk*. Biography.com. https://www.biography.com/people/elon-musk-20837159. (footnote 32)

Boboltz, S. (2017, December 7). These 13 famous companies turned out way differently than they started. *The Huffington Post*. https://www.huffingtonpost.com/2014/01/08/weird-business-origins_n_4546213.html. (footnote 50)

Bradberry, T. (2016, January 27). *Here's why every employee should have unlimited vacation days. Entrepreneur*. https://www.entrepreneur.com/article/269989. (footnote 144)

Brandson, R. (2021, July). *Richard Branson's blog: get Out of office*. Virgin.com. https://www.virgin.com/richard-branson/get-out-office. (footnote 143)

Brown, R. (2015, April 19). *Quirky needs you to return your Wink hub*. CNET. https://www.cnet.com/news/quirky-needs-your-wink-hub-back-after-a-security-update/. (footnote 5)

Buckingham, M., & Coffman, C. (2016). *First, Break All the Rules: What the World's Greatest Managers Do Differently*. Gallup Press. (footnote 91)

Campisi, J., & Said, S. (2018, July 13). *America has just one Blockbuster left*. CNN. https://www.cnn.com/2018/07/13/us/last-blockbuster-america-trnd/index.html. (footnote 23)

Carmichael, S. (2015, December 28). The research is clear: Long hours backfire for people and for companies. *Harvard Business Review*. https://hbr.org/2015/08/the-research-is-clear-long-hours-backfire-for-people-and-for-companies. (footnotes 134 & 137)

Chapin, A. (2016, June 28). *Forever 21's business has reportedly slowed way down* Racked. https://www.racked.com/2016/6/28/12051552/forever-21-business-slowdown. (footnote 61)

Cheng, A. (2013, August 19). *Forever 21 under fire for shifting full-time employees to part time.* MarketWatch. https://www.marketwatch.com/story/forever-21-under-fire-for-shifting-fulltime-employees-to-part-time-1376936367. (footnote 59)

Chou, S. (n.d.). 108: *How John Rampton lost his 7 figure Amazon business.* MyWifeQuitHerJob.com. https://mywifequitherjob.com/john-rampton-amazon-banned/. (footnote 16)

Chung, G. (2016, October 5). Exclusive interview with one of America's most successful immigrants: Forever 21's Do Won Chang. *Forbes.* https://www.forbes.com/sites/gracechung/2016/10/05/exclusive-interview-with-one-of-americas-most-successful-immigrants-forever-21s-do-won-chang/#25ad657542ab. (footnote 56)

Coffee roaster—Brewers, subscriptions & Brew guides—Blue Bottle Coffee. Coffee Roaster—Brewers, Subscriptions & Brew Guides—Blue Bottle Coffee. (n.d.). https://bluebottlecoffee.com/our-story. (footnote 51)

Cohan, P. (2013, February 27). 4 reasons Marissa Mayer's no-at-home-work policy is an epic fail. *Forbes.* https://www.forbes.com/sites/petercohan/2013/02/26/4-reasons-marissa-mayers-no-at-home-work-policy-is-an-epic-fail/?sh=2a3d0df82246. (footnote 83)

Covey, S. (2006). *The Speed of Trust.* Free Press. (footnote 108)

Cohan, P. (2016, June 22). 4 Reasons $2.86 Billion Tesla Motors/SolarCity bid is the opposite of a 'no-brainer'. *Forbes.*

https://www.forbes.com/sites/petercohan/2016/06/22/4-reasons-tesla-motorssolarcity-is-a-2-86-billion-anti-no-brainer/?sh=46a209c45fc6. (footnote 41)

Craig, S., Buettner, R., Barstow, D., & X, G. J. (2018, October 2). 4 ways Fred Trump made Donald Trump and his siblings rich. *The New York Times.* https://www.nytimes.com/interactive/2018/10/02/us/politics/trump-family-wealth.html. (footnote 78)

DeMers, J. (2018, April 3). 5 successful business leaders that have used meditation to improve productivity, creativity, and business acumen. *Business Insider.* https://www.businessinsider.com/5-successful-leaders-that-have-used-meditation-to-be-more-productive-2018-4. (footnote 146)

Detrick, H. (2021, June 8). United Airlines CEO deferred his bonus to show 'accountability and integrity' but he still made $10M. *Fortune.* http://fortune.com/2018/04/24/united-airlines-ceo-bonus/. (footnote 74)

DeWolf, D. (2021, April 24). How this CEO regained trust with his employees. *Fortune.* http://fortune.com/2015/07/30/david-dewolf-building-trust/. (footnote 66)

DollarShaveClub. (2012, March 6). *DollarShaveClub.com—our blades are f***ing great* [Video]. YouTube. https://www.youtube.com/watch?v=ZUG9qYTJMsI&t=1s. (footnote 97)

Dean, J. (2013, September 30). Is this the world's most creative manufacturer? *Inc.* https://www.inc.com/magazine/201310/josh-dean/is-quirky-the-worlds-most-creative-manufacturer.html. (footnote 1)

D'Onfro, J. (2015, April 29). How a quirky 28-year-old plowed through $150 million and almost destroyed his start-up. *Business Insider.* https://www.businessinsider. com/quirky-ben-kaufman-2015-4. (footnote 2)

D'Onfro, J. (2015, June 13). Fresh funding and more departures at Quirky, the New York startup that burned through $150 million. *Business Insider.* https://www.businessinsider.com/quirky-funding-and-changes-2015-6. (footnote 8)

Duerr, S. (2017, August). They help women move—literally—out of abusive relationships. *Miami Herald.* https://www.miamiherald.com/news/nation-world/national/article164779607.html. (footnote 103)

Estrada, Z. (2018, February 7). *Tesla burns through $2 billion in 2017.* The Verge. https://www.theverge.com/2018/2/7/16986396/tesla-2017-full-year-earnings-model-3-production. (footnote 34)

Fabricant, F. (2017, December 29). Guy Fieri says farewell to Times Square. *The New York Times.* https://www.nytimes.com/2017/12/29/dining/guy-fieri-restaurant-closing.html. (footnote 125)

Farr, C. (2015, October). Why Homejoy failed. *Wired.* https://www.wired.com/2015/10/why-homejoy-failed/. (footnotes 111, 112 & 114)

Feintzeig, R. (2009, September 29). Jolt Cola looks to recharge in bankruptcy. *The Wall Street Journal.* https://blogs.wsj.com/bankruptcy/2009/09/29/jolt-cola-looks-to-recharge-in-bankruptcy/. (footnote 118)

Fickenscher, L. (2016, April 29). Forever 21 is having problems paying the bills. *New York Post.* https://nypost.com/2016/04/28/forever-21-is-having-problems-paying-the-bills/. (footnote 60)

Fieri, G. (n.d.). *Guy Fieri's Top Recipes.* Food Network. https://www.foodnetwork.com/profiles/talent/guy-fieri/guy-fieris-top-recipes. (footnote 124)

Fleishman, G. (2021, June 8). Musk honors flint pledge: Donates cash to bring clean water to city's schools. *Fortune.* http://fortune.com/2018/10/08/musk-gives-clean-water-flint-schools/. (footnote 151)

Franck, T. (2018, January 24). *Analyst jokes Musk will make it to Mars with SpaceX before Tesla is profitable.* CNBC. https://www.cnbc.com/2017/11/28/analyst-jokes-musk-will-make-it-to-mars-before-tesla-is-profitable.html. (footnote 38)

Fung, B. (2019, April 8). This is why Elon Musk is buying SolarCity. *The Washington Post.* https://www.washingtonpost.com/news/the-switch/wp/2016/06/22/this-is-why-elon-musk-is-buying-solarcity/. (footnote 39)

Gelles, D. (2018, September 21). *Mark Bertolini of Aetna on yoga, meditation and Darth Vader.* The New York Times. Retrieved November 5, 2021, from https://www.nytimes.com/2018/09/21/business/mark-bertolini-aetna-corner-office.html. (footnote 148)

Gladwell, Malcolm. "The Sure Thing." *The New Yorker*, 11 Jan. 2010, https://www.newyorker.com/magazine/2010/01/18/the-sure-thing (footnote 67)

Gleason, S., & Mann, T. (2015, December 4). GE says Quirky has hurt its reputation. *The Wall Street Journal.* https://www.wsj.com/articles/ge-says-quirky-has-hurt-its-reputation-1449179311. (footnotes 7 & 10)

Goel, V. (2016, January 10). Yahoo's brain drain shows a loss of faith inside the company. *The New York Times.* https://www.nytimes.com/2016/01/11/technology/yahoos-

brain-drain-shows-a-loss-of-faith-inside-the-company.
html_r=0. (footnote 86)

Goldman, D. (2016, July 25). *Jerry and David's guide to
the World Wide Web.* CNNMoney. http://money.cnn.
com/gallery/technology/2015/03/03/yahoo-20-years-hits-
flops/10.html. (footnote 80)

Goodreads. (n.d.). *A quote from bad science.* Goodreads.
Retrieved November 5, 2021, from https://www.
goodreads.com/quotes/3051240-fooling-around-with-
alternating-current-is-just-a-waste-of. (footnote 106)

Graser, M. (2013, December 8). Epic fail: How Blockbuster
could have owned Netflix. *Variety.* https://variety.
com/2013/biz/news/epic-fail-how-blockbuster-could-
have-owned- netflix-1200823443/. (footnotes 20 & 22)

Greenfield. R. (2013, October 30). It's hard out there for a
venture capitalist. *The Atlantic.* https://www.theatlantic.
com/technology/archive/2012/08/its-hard-out-there-
venture-capitalist/324377/. (footnote 53)

Griffith, E. (2017, January 13). Buzzfeed wants to sell you
stuff. *Fortune.* http://fortune.com/2016/11/21/buzzfeed-
commerce-ben-kaufman/. (footnote 11)

Gunther, M. (2015, January). *Is it okay to bring your heart
to work?* Collaboration Business Consulting. https://
collaboration-llc.com/is-it-okay-to-bring-your-heart-
into-work/. (footnote 101)

Guzior, B. (n.d.). *Google staff meeting canceled; memo debate
rages on.* Bizjournals.com. https://www.bizjournals.
com/bizwomen/news/latest-news/2017/08/google-staff-
meeting-canceled-memo-debate-rages-on.html?page=all.
(footnote 94)

Handy. (n.d.). *About Us*. Handy. Retrieved November 5, 2021, from https://www.glassdoor.com/Overview/Working-at-Handy-EI_IE680570.11,16.htm (footnote 115)

Hardy, Q. (2015, March 20). At Kodak, clinging to a future beyond film. *The New York Times*. https://www.nytimes.com/2015/03/22/business/at-kodak-clinging-to-a-future-beyond-film.html. (footnote 76)

Harter, J. (2021, August 5). *Employee engagement on the rise in the U.S.* Gallup.com. https://news.gallup.com/poll/241649/employee-engagement-rise.aspx. (footnote 89)

Higginbotham, S. (2015, September 22). Quirky files for bankruptcy and accepts $15 million bid on wink from Flextronics. *Fortune*. http://fortune.com/2015/09/22/quirky-files-bankruptcy/. (footnote 9)

Hiskey, D. (2012, November 28). *Robert Downey Jr. modeled his portrayal of Tony Stark After Elon MUSK, one of the founders of Zip2, Paypal, Tesla Motors, SolarCity, and SpaceX*. Today I Found Out. https://www.todayifoundout.com/index.php/2011/08/robert-downey-jr-modeled-his-portrayal-of-tony-stark-after-elon-musk-one-of-the-founders-of-zip2-paypal-tesla-motors-and-spacex/. (footnote 33)

Holmes, R. (2017, January 31). Why it's time we paid people to exercise at work. *Inc*. https://www.inc.com/linkedin/ryan-holmes/why-its-time-we-paid-employees-exercise-work-ryan-holmes.html. (footnote 147)

Horta-Osório, A. (2018, May 1). It's time to end the workplace taboo around mental Health | António Horta-Osório. *The Guardian*. https://www.theguardian.com/commentisfree/2018/may/01/removeing-taboo-mental-health-work-lloyds-banking-group-antonio-horta-osorio. (footnotes 139 & 141)

"If Your Work Is Done, Why Wait?" *Professor Walter's History Lessons*, https://www.professorwalter.com/2012/01/if-your-work-is-done-why-wait.html (footnote 77)

Isaacson, W. (2014). *The Innovators*. Simon & Schuster Ltd. (footnote 25)

Isidore, C. (2018, October 26). *Meet the New, profitable, Tesla*. CNN Business. https://www.cnn.com/2018/10/26/tech/tesla-profit/index.html. (footnote 35)

James, G. (2012, April 24). Lessons from Sheryl Sandberg: Stop working more than 40 hours a week. *Inc.* https://www.inc.com/geoffrey-james/stop-working-more-than-40-hours-a-week.html. (footnote 136)

Jhonsa, E. (2019, January 4). *Netflix still has a good growth story, despite potential near-term turbulence*. TheStreet. https://www.thestreet.com/technology/netflix-good-growth-story-despite-turbulence-14824501. (footnote 24)

Kass, K. (2012, March 27). *Best Buy—town hall meetings*. Inline Multimedia Production. http://www.inlineproductions.com/best-buy-town-hall-meetings/. (footnote 95)

Kelly, M. (2018, January 17). *Daniel Pink's 'when' shows the importance of timing throughout life*. NPR. https://www.npr.org/2018/01/17/578666036/daniel-pinks-when-shows-the-importance-of-timing-throughout-life. (footnote 65)

Kieler, A. (2016, September 28). *New United CEO apologizes for 5 years of merger-related problems*. Consumerist. https://consumerist.com/2015/10/01/new-united-ceo-apologizes-for-5-years-of-merger-related-problems/. (footnote 71)

Klein, A. (2015, June 11). *Red Bull drinkers can claim $10 over 'gives you wings' lawsuit.* NBCNews. https://www.nbcnews.com/business/consumer/red-bull-drinkers-can-claim-10-over-gives- you-wings-n221901. (footnote 120)

Kwan, W., Pham, T., & Kiander, T. (2020, December 9). *Diminishing returns—working more does not mean getting more done.* Asian Efficiency. https://www.asianefficiency.com/mindsets/diminishing-returns-working-more-does-not-mean-getting-more-done/. (footnote 135)

Lagorio-Chafkin, Christine. "The Lesson Management Guru Jim Collins Learned from Steve Jobs." *Inc.com*, Inc., 25 Jan. 2021, https://www.inc.com/christine-lagorio/jim-collins-steve-jobs-apple-what-i-know-podcast.html. (footnotes 13 & 27)

Larcker, D. F., Miles, S., Tayan, B., & Gutman, M. E. (2013, August 1). *2013 executive coaching survey.* Stanford Graduate School of Business. https://www.gsb.stanford.edu/faculty-research/publications/2013-executive-coaching-survey. (footnote 28)

Laroya, L. M. M. (2014, October 10). *These highly successful people tell you to take vacations from work.* Lifehack. https://www.lifehack.org/articles/work/these-highly-successful-people-tell-you-take-vacations-from-work.html. (footnote 145)

Lashinsky, A. (2015, March 10). How Dollar Shave Club got started. *Fortune.* http://fortune.com/2015/03/10/dollar-shave-club-founding/. (footnote 98)

Leadership Pipeline Institute. (n.d.). https://leadershippipelineinstitute.com/resources. (footnote 70)

Leinwand, P., Mainardi, C., & Kleiner, A. (2020, September 11). Only 8% of leaders are good at both strategy and execution. *Harvard Business Review.* https://hbr.org/2015/12/only-8-of-leaders-are-good-at-both-strategy-and-execution. (footnote 130)

LeSage, J. (2017, December 23). Electric vehicles: Toyota could become Tesla's next big headache. *USA Today.* https://www.usatoday.com/story/money/energy/2017/12/23/electric-vehicles-toyota-could-become-teslas-next-big-headache/977877001/. (footnote 37)

Lidow, D. (2019, September 11). Why two-thirds of the fastest-growing companies fail. *Fortune.* http://fortune.com/2016/03/07/fast-growth-companies-fail/. (footnote 131)

Mansfield, M. (2021, January 23). *Startup statistics—the numbers you need to know.* Small Business Trends. https://smallbiztrends.com/2016/11/startup-statistics-small-business.html. (footnotes 54 & 109)

Matthews Fan Company, https://matthewsfan.com/about-us/ (footnote 47)

Mejia, Z. (2017, June 1). *Why Marissa Mayer is the 'least likable' CEO in tech.* CNBC. https://www.cnbc.com/2017/05/31/why-yahoo-ceo-marissa-mayer-is-the-least-likable-ceo-in-tech.html. (footnote 85)

Mental Health UK. (2019, April 24). *Lloyds banking group joins forces with Mental Health UK.* Mental Health UK. https://mentalhealth-uk.org/blog/lloyds-banking-group-joins-forces-with-mental-health-uk/. (footnote 140)

Meyer, D. (2021, June 8). Here's what you need to know About SpaceX's satellite broadband plans. *Fortune.*

http://fortune.com/2018/02/22/spacex-starlink-satellite-broadband/. (footnote 31)

Myatt, Mike. "Marissa Mayer: A Case Study in Poor Leadership." *Forbes*, Forbes Magazine, 13 Dec. 2015, https://www.forbes.com/sites/mikemyatt/2015/11/20/marissa-mayer-case-study-in-poor-leadership/?sh=1f730e3a3b46 (footnote 87)

O'Kane, S. (2018, March 10). *Tesla's toughest competition ever was on display in Geneva.* The Verge. https://www.theverge.com/2018/3/10/17096608/tesla-jaguar-porsche-audi-evs-geneva-motor-show-2018. (footnote 36)

Overfield, D., & Kaiser, R. (2020, April 23). One out of every two managers is terrible at accountability. *Harvard Business Review.* https://hbr.org/2012/11/one-out-of-every-two-managers-is-terrible-at-accountability. (footnote 107)

Patel, N. (2015, October 22). 6 things that entrepreneurs did before they became entrepreneurs. *Inc.* https://www.inc.com/neil-patel/6-things-that-entrepreneurs-did-before-they-became-entrepreneurs.html. (footnote 110)

Patel, S. (2015, January 29). 5 myths about building a million-dollar business. *Forbes.* https://www.forbes.com/sites/theyec/2015/01/28/5-myths-about-building-a-million-dollar-business/ (footnote 79)

Perez, S. (2018, August 30). *Walmart.com now sells Handy's installation and assembly services.* TechCrunch. https://techcrunch.com/2018/08/30/walmart-com-now-sells-handys-installation-and-assembly-services/. (footnote 116)

Perlroth, N. (2017, October 3). All 3 billion Yahoo accounts were affected by 2013 attack. *The New York Times.*

https://www.nytimes.com/2017/10/03/technology/yahoo-hack-3-billion-users.html. (footnote 88)

Petroff, A. (n.d.). *Boring company: Elon Musk says he has sold out of flamethrowers.* CNNMoney. https://money.cnn.com/2018/02/01/technology/flamethrower-elon-musk-boring-company-sold-out/index.html. (footnote 30)

Pixar's 22 rules of storytelling. (2013, March 7). Aerogramme Writer's Studio. Retrieved September 8, 2021, from https://www.aerogrammestudio.com/2013/03/07/pixars-22-rules-of-storytelling/ (footnote 100)

Primack, D. (2021, April 25). Unilever buys Dollar Shave Club for $1 billion. *Fortune.* http://fortune.com/2016/07/19/unilever-buys-dollar-shave-club-for-1-billion/. (footnote 99)

Pofeldt, Elaine. "Why Dal Lamagna of Tweezer-Man Deferred Retirement to Steer Recovery of Icestone." *Inc.com*, Inc., 5 May 2014, https://www.inc.com/magazine/201405/elain-pofeldt/dal-lamagna-hurricane-sandy-recovery-empowered-employees.html (footnote 69)

Primack, D., & Higginbotham, S. (2015, June 12). Exclusive: Quirky ditches device manufacturing, preps for new investment. *Fortune.* http://fortune.com/2015/06/12/quirky-wink-funding-products/. (footnote 6)

Quirky (2015, April 23). *Quirky: Live product evaluation.* YouTube. https://www.youtube.com/watch?v=3TTEMnFMkOc. (footnotes 3 & 4)

Radke, B. (2014, April 16). *Talking big flavors and Big Vegas openings with Guy Fieri.* Las Vegas Weekly. Retrieved November 5, 2021, from https://lasvegasweekly.com/dining/chef-talk/2014/apr/16/talking-big-flavors-and-big-vegas-openings-guy-fie/. (footnote 127)

Rampton, J. (2016, July 12). 8 ways my ego killed my business. *Entrepreneur.* https://www.entrepreneur.com/article/278901#. (footnotes 15 & 29)

Red Bull. (n.d.). *Giving wiiings to people and ideas.* RedBull.com https://energydrink-us.redbull.com/en/company. (footnote 121)

Sauers, J. (2011, July 20). *How forever 21 keeps getting away with designer knockoffs.* Jezebel. https://jezebel.com/5822762/how-forever-21-keeps-getting-away-with-designer-knockoffs. (footnote 57)

Schultz, E. J. (2017, September 8). *Wake up America: Jolt cola is coming back.* Ad Age. http://adage.com/article/cmo-strategy/wake-america-jolt-cola-coming-back/310399/. (footnote 117)

Segal, D. (2012, March 19). Chaleo Yoovidhya, who created Red Bull beverage, is dead. *The New York Times.* https://www.nytimes.com/2012/03/19/business/chaleo-yoovidhya-dies-created-red-bull-energy-drink.html. (footnote 119)

Segall, L. (2017, August 10). *Google CEO cancels town hall due to leaks.* CNNMoney. http://money.cnn.com/2017/08/10/technology/business/google-meeting-questions/index.html. (footnote 93)

Shapiro, Stephen. "Stop Worrying about the Novelty of Your Ideas." *Inc.com*, Inc., 22 Aug. 2020, https://www.inc.com/stephen-shapiro/stop-worrying-about-novelty-of-your-ideas. (footnote 96)

Sharpe, K. (2016, September 7). On the Via Francigena in Tuscany, monasteries and fellowship. *The New York Times.* https://www.nytimes.com/2016/09/11/travel/via-francigena-tuscany.html. (footnote 153)

Shontell, A (2010, December 29). How 15 failed businesses led one Founder to a multi-million-dollar success. *Business Insider.* https://www.businessinsider.com/how-15-failed-businesses-led-the-founder-of-tweezerman-to-a-multi-million-dollar-empire-2010-12. (footnote 68)

Siu, E. (2015, February 14). Surprising lessons from companies that failed despite a fail-proof product. *Forbes.* https://www.forbes.com/sites/theyec/2014/09/18/surprising-lessons-from-companies-that-failed-despite-a-fail-proof-product/ (footnote 122)

Smith, J. (2018, July 18). Inside FreshDirect's big bet to win the home-delivery fight. *The Wall Street Journal.* https://www.wsj.com/articles/inside-the-food-fight-over-home-delivery-1531906200. (footnote 123)

Smith, R. (2017, February 5). *How profitable is SpaceX, really?* The Motley Fool. https://www.fool.com/investing/2017/02/05/how-profitable-is-spacex-really.aspx. (footnote 43)

The state of US venture capital in 15 charts. PitchBook. (n.d.). https://pitchbook.com/news/articles/the-state-of-us-venture-capital-activity-in-15-charts. (footnote 52)

Stillman, J. (2012, April 9). Sheryl Sandberg leaves work at 5:30. Why can't you? Inc. https://www.inc.com/jessica-stillman/facebook-sheryl-sandberg-can-leave-early-why-arent-you.html. (footnote 142)

Sytsma, A. (2012, November 15). *Guy Fieri responds to smackdown.* Grub Street. Retrieved November 5, 2021, from https://www.grubstreet.com/2012/11/guy-fieri-responds-to-restaurant-review.html. (footnote 128)

Trex, E. (2013, August 20). *15 famous companies that originally sold something else.* Mental Floss. http://

mentalfloss.com/article/22822/15-companies-originally-sold-something-else. (footnote 49)

Tyler, J. (2018, June 7). We shopped at Forever 21 and H&M to see which was a better fast-fashion store, and the winner was clear for a key reason. *Business Insider.* https://www.businessinsider.com/forever-21-hm-which-is-better-2018-6. (footnote 63)

Tynan, D. (2020, June 2). *The history of Yahoo, and how it went from phenom to has-been.* Fast Company. https://www.fastcompany.com/40544277/the-glory-that-was-yahoo. (footnote 81)

Ungerleider, N. (2015, September 22) "Quirky Files for Bankruptcy, Agrees to Sell Smart Home Subsidiary Wink." *Fast Company,* https://www.fastcompany.com/3051418/quirky-files-for-bankruptcy-agrees-to-sell-smart-home-subsidiary-wink?cid=search (footnote 12)

Urbaniak, M. (2016, July 19). *PODCAST: "Failure Is an Epic Part of Success" with John Rampton.* Brand24. com. https://brand24.com/blog/failure-epic-part-success-john-rampton/. (footnote 14)

US Travel Association. (2019, October 18). *State of American vacation 2018.* U.S. Travel Association. https://projecttimeoff.com/reports/state-of-american-vacation-2018/. (footnote 133)

US Travel Association. (2021, May 27). *Time off and vacation usage.* U.S. Travel Association. https://projecttimeoff.com/blog/doctors-orders-take-a-vacation/. (footnote 138)

Valdes-Dapena, P. (n.d.). *Tesla's $200,000 Roadster will need more than record-breaking speed.* CNNMoney. http://money.cnn.com/2017/11/17/technology/tesla-roadster/index.html. (footnote 40)

VanHemert, K. (2015, March 24). How Steve Jobs tamed his explosive genius. *Wired*. https://www.wired.com/2015/03/steve-jobs-tamed-explosive-genius/. (footnote 26)

Vintage Value Investing. (2017, November 6). Warren Buffett's best investing advice for beginners. *Business Insider*. http://www.businessinsider.com/warren-buffett-best-investing-advice-for-beginners-2017-11. (footnote 45)

Webster, A. (2007, September 4). When a fight for more money is also a battle for dignity. *The New York Times*. https://www.nytimes.com/2007/09/04/arts/television/04docu.html. (footnote 58)

Weinberger, M. (2020, February 11). The rise and fall of Marissa Mayer, the once-beloved CEO of Yahoo now pursuing her own venture. *Business Insider*. http://www.businessinsider.com/yahoo-marissa-mayer-rise-and-fall-2017-6. (footnote 82)

Weintraub, S. (2010, September 30). Excite passed up buying Google for $750,000 in 1999. *Fortune*. http://fortune.com/2010/09/29/excite-passed-up-buying-google-for-750000-in-1999/. (footnote 21)

Wells, P. (2012, November 13). As not seen on TV. *The New York Times*. https://www.nytimes.com/2012/11/14/dining/reviews/restaurant-review-guys-american-kitchen-bar-in-times-square.html. (footnotes 126 & 129)

Wickre, K. (2017, August 16). What Google's open communication culture is really like. *Wired*. https://www.wired.com/story/what-googles-open-communication-culture-is-really-like/. (footnote 92)

Wikimedia Foundation. (2021, August 12). *List of assets owned by Berkshire Hathaway*. Wikipedia. https://

en.wikipedia.org/wiki/List_of_assets_owned_by_
Berkshire_Hathaway. (footnote 46)

Winkler, R., & Pasztor, A. (2017, January 13). Exclusive peek
at SpaceX data shows loss in 2015, heavy expectations for
nascent internet service. *The Wall Street Journal*. https://
www.wsj.com/articles/exclusive-peek-at-spacex-data-
shows-loss-in-2015-heavy-expectations-for-nascent-
internet-service-1484316455. (footnote 42)

Wisner, F. (2012). *Edelman and the rise of public relations*.
Daniel J. Edelman, Inc. (footnote 55)

Wong, K. (2018, June 12). Dealing with impostor syndrome
when you're treated as an impostor. *The New York Times*.
https://www.nytimes.com/2018/06/12/smarter-living/
dealing-with-impostor-syndrome-when-youre-treated-
as-an-impostor.html. (footnote 132)

Woolsey, B. (2015, December 6). Meathead Movers offers
services for free to victims of domestic abuse. *Los
Angeles Times*. https://www.latimes.com/socal/daily-
pilot/tn-wknd-et-1206-meathead-movers-20151206-
story.html. (footnote 102)

Wpcurve.com, https://wpcurve.com/homejoy-adora-cheung/
(footnote 113)

"Worst Tech Predictions of All Time." *The Telegraph*,
Telegraph Media Group, 29 June 2016, https://www.
telegraph.co.uk/technology/0/worst-tech-predictions-of-
all-time/youtube-founders/. (footnote 105)

Yarow, Jay. "Here's What Steve Ballmer Thought about
the Iphone Five Years Ago." *Business Insider*, Business
Insider, 29 June 2012, https://www.businessinsider.com/
heres-what-steve-ballmer-thought-about-the-iphone-five-
years-ago-2012. (footnote 104)

Yeh, C. (2015, July 24). What Marissa Mayer got wrong (and right) about stack ranking employees. *Harvard Business Review.* https://hbr.org/2015/01/what-marissa-mayer-got-wrong-and-right-about-stack-ranking-employees. (footnote 84)

Yohn, D. L. (2018, April 2). How to fix United Airlines' culture problem. *Forbes.* https://www.forbes.com/sites/deniselyohn/2018/03/28/how-to-fix-united-airlines-culture-problem/. (footnotes 72 & 73)

Zak, P. (2019, November 27). The neuroscience of trust. *Harvard Business Review.* https://hbr.org/2017/01/the-neuroscience-of-trust. (footnote 90)

Zdanowicz, C. (2018, October 9). *Flint schools are getting safe water fountains thanks to Elon Musk.* CNN. https://www.cnn.com/2018/10/08/us/elon-musk-flint-schools-water-filtration-trnd/index.html. (footnote 152)

Zhou, L. (2018, July 18). *Elon Musk and the Thai cave rescue: A tale of good intentions and bad tweets.* Vox. https://www.vox.com/2018/7/18/17576302/elon-musk-thai-cave-rescue-submarine. (footnotes 149 & 150)

www.ingramcontent.com/pod-product-compliance
Lightning Source LLC
Chambersburg PA
CBHW042116190326
41519CB00030B/7513